UNSOLVED MICHIGAN

UNSOLVED MICHIGAN

NINA INNSTED

THE History PRESS

Published by The History Press
An imprint of Arcadia Publishing
Charleston, SC
www.historypress.com

First published 2026

Manufactured in the United States

ISBN 9781467159333
Hardcover ISBN 9781540299567

Library of Congress Control Number applied for.

CONTENTS

ACKNOWLEDGEMENTS

A project like this doesn't happen without the help and support of family; without them, this work would not be possible.

Thanks also go out to the many law enforcement agencies I connected with—the Livingston County Sheriff's Department Cold Case team, the Midland County Sheriff's Department, White Lake Township Police, Farmington Public Safety, Shiawassee County Sheriff's Office, Marquette Police, St. Clair Shores Police, and the Macomb County Sheriff's Office—and countless others who answered questions and kept me pointed in the right direction.

Thanks to the families and friends who were kind enough to speak with me about their loved ones: Nikki, Michele, Georgia, Mesha, Kimberly, Teigha, Joe, Brandon, Kathie, Konnie, Annie, Gina, Pamela, Carrie, and others.

Thank you also to John for answering every question with good grace.

Thanks also to my "framily." I am blessed beyond measure.

INTRODUCTION

After almost a decade of my writing about Michigan and Great Lakes–centric true crime cases for the *Already Gone* podcast and more than seven years spent volunteering with the Missing in Michigan organization, this book could have included dozens, if not hundreds, of cases.

So many of these people don't get enough mention, from the 1988 case of Lincoln Park's Phyllis Flynn—twenty-three-year-old Flynn went to Detroit for a romantic interlude and never returned—to the baffling disappearance of seventeen year-old Perry Corlew, who took off following a fender bender in Grayling. Corlew's car, a 1971 Buick Skylark, was recovered, but the six-foot, three-inch teenager was never seen again.

Each of these cases and each of these people is important. They and their families deserve justice and answers.

Sometimes the best you can do is share their stories.

PART I
THE MURDERED

1
AKITA ERVIN
1992

Was Akita Ervin a wild child? You might say Akita was difficult, free-spirited, or troubled. If you are going to say these things about her, let's also talk about nature versus nurture. Akita didn't have a stable upbringing. The way that she was raised, the attention, or lack of attention, or the wrong kind of attention she received throughout her short life, molded her and influenced her choices.

In the police file about her case, there are stories about Akita running with crackheads in Pontiac and tales of young Akita drinking alcohol and smoking marijuana in parking lots.

When Akita was home with her mother, the one place she should have felt safe and loved, it wasn't a good place to be. Akita reportedly told friends that she was avoiding inappropriate attention from her mother's live-in boyfriend.

While Akita's mom, Diana Ervin, was off at work on an overnight shift, Akita was left alone with a man who made her uncomfortable, a man who allegedly offered her drugs and vacillated between being an inappropriate creeper and a paternal figure.

Akita did not have a warm relationship with her mother; they argued and there was conflict between them. Her childhood was punctuated by her mother's romantic entanglements, which saw Akita being sent to live with a relative or family friend for weeks or even months at a time on the whim of her mother or her mother's boyfriends. Akita's relationship with her father wasn't much better. She saw him infrequently.

A young Akita Ervin. *Ervin family.*

Before we explore Akita's story further, do not forget that no one mentioned in this story was ever arrested, charged, or named a person of interest in her case.

As we go forward, remember that Akita can't give you her side of the story; she can't tell you about her experiences, her choices, or why she ran away from home time and again. She can't tell you because someone silenced her, making sure that Akita could never reveal their secrets.

Akita Rochelle Ervin was born on July 8, 1976, to Diana Ervin and her boyfriend Abraham Watkins. At the time of Akita's birth, Diana was single and still in her teens. We don't know if Ervin and Watkins were romantically involved when Akita was born, but Akita was his daughter and Watkins had visitation and paid child support. He loved Akita.

Akita and her mother spent many years living in the city of Pontiac, the same city her father called home. Diana Ervin moved with Akita out of Pontiac after she became involved with Gary France* (not his real name).[1]

Diana became involved with France when Akita was around ten years old. Akita was not in favor of moving. She wanted to stay put; she had friends in the neighborhood and friends at school. Diana was pursuing her relationship with Gary France, so she and Akita moved in with France, the three of them sharing a mobile home in White Lake Township.

Akita did not like living in White Lake. She was a city girl and missed Pontiac. Gary, her mother's boyfriend, later told police that Akita "ran with the crackheads" and sometimes ran away from their home to return to Pontiac. He told police that once she walked from their home to Pontiac, a distance of more than ten miles. Sometimes, while in Pontiac, she stayed with her dad or with friends. At other times, she stayed with whomever welcomed her in. These were not always good people, and Akita was known to lie about her age, presenting herself as much older than her fifteen years.

In March and April 1992, Akita ran away from home. Her high school principal, Sam Osbourne, told police that Akita last attended school on

February 25, and by March 12, she had been entered into the school's system as a runaway. While Akita didn't return to classes, she was last seen at school on May 21, when she and her mother came in to register her for the fall term. When pressed for additional information about Akita, Principal Osborne stated that Akita was unhappy at home and did not like her mother's boyfriend.

While Akita was miserable living with her mother and Gary in White Lake, she wasn't any happier when she stayed with her father in Pontiac.

On June 10, 1992, Diana Ervin arrived home from work after her night shift and went straight to bed. She did not check in on Akita. It's believed that when she awoke on the afternoon of the tenth, she noticed that Akita wasn't home. Diana did not make any calls to locate her daughter. The eleventh passed and then the twelfth, Diana's birthday.

Akita never returned to the home she shared with her mother and Gary France. She did not contact her grandmother, her father, or any of her friends. There was not only no sign of her but also no alarm sounded over her absence.

On June 22, 1992, a local man was taking a walk through the woods in White Lake, about half a mile from the trailer where Akita Ervin lived with her mother and her "stepdad."

This man, Lee Montgomery*, smelled something awful in the woods and walked farther in to see if he could determine the source of the putrid odor. He entered a small clearing and realized there was a body. He saw hands and feet. Montgomery immediately left for home, where he called the police to report what he'd found.

When an officer responded to the scene, following Montgomery into the woods, the policeman confirmed that it was indeed human remains, and he radioed back to the station. He wanted to advise the chief and the detective bureau of the discovery. When the investigative team arrived, they immediately began taking pictures and gathering evidence, including cigarette butts and other items found near the remains.

The body was carefully removed from the location and taken to the medical examiner in Pontiac for processing. It was determined to be a Black female, approximately five feet, six inches tall, 105 pounds. She was wearing only underwear. There was a great deal of insect activity, and the remains were distorted from decomposition. The medical examiner gave the estimated time of death as one to three weeks earlier. He listed the cause of death as blunt force trauma to the neck.

While the medical examiner was attending to the remains, officers searched the scene with metal detectors, collecting additional evidence.

Back at the station, police began looking for missing person reports and found one that looked promising: a missing person's report for Akita Rochelle Ervin from April 4, 1992. When police contacted Akita's mother, Diana, she said that Akita had returned home in April but was missing again.

Remember, it was June 22. Diana told police that Akita went missing on June 11. That's almost two weeks without contact from her daughter. During this time, Diana did not place worried calls to Akita's father, or grandmother. She didn't call Akita's friends to ask if anyone had seen her. She didn't call the police to ask for assistance in locating her missing child.

When asked by law enforcement, Diana Ervin provided the name of Akita's dentist. When police contacted the dentist, the office confirmed that Akita was treated on May 28, 1992. The dentist and the forensic odontologist at the medical examiner's office connected, and using dental records, her identity was confirmed. The body in the woods was Akita Ervin.

Police went to the mobile home Akita shared with her mother and Gary France. They advised Diana that her daughter was no longer missing and asked her to come to the station with them.

Akita was laid to rest just days after her remains were found. Her grave is marked with a heart-shaped memorial featuring a photo of Akita and engravings of praying hands, a theatrical mask, and the Disney character Goofy.

Akita's headstone at the Oak Hill Cemetery in Pontiac. *Author's collection.*

In an interview after Akita's death, her father, Abraham Watkins, told police that he had not seen his daughter since the first week of May. Later in May, he saw Akita's mother at a Friend of the Court hearing at the Oakland County Court in Pontiac.

Watkins told police that Akita was known to use drugs, that she was running with older boys, and that teenagers and men, including men who were locked up in jail, called his home looking for Akita. He told police that Akita was on good terms with his live-in girlfriend, Daysha*. Akita confided in Daysha.

Akita told Daysha that Gary France touched her inappropriately. France offered her drugs and alcohol, and Akita wanted to get away from him, but when she talked to her mom about feeling unsafe around her "stepdad," France lied about what had happened and her mother didn't believe her.

Akita's status as a biracial student certainly played a part in her ability to fit in and feel comfortable while living in White Lake. Akita was one of the few African American students at her school. It's worth considering that Akita didn't feel comfortable being a nonwhite teenager in the primarily white community.

In Pontiac, with her African American father, she was just another Black child, and it appears she felt more comfortable in the city. According to Wikipedia, in 2000, White Lake was 96 percent white and less than 1 percent African American. On the other hand, in the 2000 census, Pontiac was about 35 percent white and 52 percent African American.

There was a period around 1988 when another couple, Suzy and Alan*, took Akita into their home. They had guardianship of Akita, and she stayed with them for several months. While staying there, she did run away, but only twice. Suzy and Alan described her as a good kid who ran with a tough crowd. They told police that Akita was looking for love and sought it out in the wrong places and from the wrong people. In 1988, Akita was only eleven years old, and she was already running away from home.

The couple also relayed to police that when Akita ran away, Diana always called to ask if they'd seen her. But this time, the last time she disappeared, there was no phone call from Diana. Akita was gone, but Diana didn't phone friends or family to ask if they had seen her. Suzy and Alan found that strange and concerning, especially when Akita had been missing for so long.

This couple advised police that they would not be surprised if France harmed Akita, and they said that France's stepdad was a sheriff's deputy. France once boasted, long before Akita's murder, that he knew how to easily beat a polygraph by taking certain drugs and using mental tricks.

When police asked if they had ever seen France be violent with Akita or Diana, they said no, but they'd been told that France once tried to run Diana over with his car during an argument.

One of Akita's neighbors in White Lake was interviewed by police. Pattie Clark* told police that Diana Ervin was unstable. She said Diana was jealous of her young, attractive daughter and the two fought often. She described a highly toxic and unstable home life for Akita, one where mother and daughter frequently had physical altercations.

In Clark's opinion, Diana Ervin was capable of murdering Akita or covering up if someone else killed her. Clark also told police that she saw Akita sitting outside on June 13, which is the day after Diana and France said Akita ran away from home.

Pattie Clark had one more bit of information for the police. In the days after Akita's funeral, Akita's maternal grandmother, Marjorie Smith, stopped by Clark's house to talk. During the visit, Smith wept about her grandchild and lamented the fact that Diana did not seem to be grieving Akita.

Kiara Bowen* was one of Akita's friends. Bowen had slept over at Akita's house a few times, and while the girls were friends, they didn't speak on the phone often because the calls were long-distance, or zone calls, which made for expensive conversations.

Kiara called for Akita on June 17, 1992, and Diana answered the phone. Diana told her that Akita had "stepped out." Kiara asked if Akita had run away again, and Diana responded, "Not exactly." Keep in mind that Akita's body was discovered only days later.

Kiara asked the police if they knew how Akita died, and they told her they didn't yet have a cause of death. Her remains were badly decomposed when she was found. Kiara told detectives that it probably wasn't a Pontiac person who killed Akita. When the police pressed her to explain, she said no one from Pontiac would drive to White Lake with a body in their car, only to dump her within a mile of her home. She also told police that Pontiac people didn't know where Akita lived in White Lake.

On July 22, 1992, detectives interviewed Raquel Powell, who lived near Akita's father in Pontiac. Powell confirmed to police that Akita and her mother fought frequently. Akita had called Powell crying on more than one occasion because Diana had thrown a bottle or an ashtray at her. On one memorable evening, Diana Ervin got so angry at Akita that she allegedly grabbed a knife and chased her out of the house.

On July 29, 1992, Diana Ervin was interviewed at the White Lake Township Police Station. She started the interview by complaining about Akita's father, Abraham "Abe" Watkins. Ervin told the police that Watkins showed up at Gary France's place of work and told his coworkers that France murdered Akita and that France had molested her. Diana was upset about Abe's actions that day.

Police asked her about the marijuana and cocaine they found in her home when they searched it after Akita's murder. She told them that she didn't smoke marijuana, and while she had used cocaine a few times, she preferred nicotine, caffeine, and liquor. The cocaine was old; France got it at a party a long time ago. Diana told police she kept a lock on her bedroom door to keep Akita out of their stuff.

Police asked when she last saw Akita, and Diana said June 9 or 10. She knew she and her mother went to Kroger to do some shopping with Akita, and she thought that it was June 9. Diana reminded them that her birthday was on June 12, and she knew Akita was gone by that point because she hadn't seen her on her birthday. Police told her that witnesses in the neighborhood saw Diana with Akita after June 12, and Diana said they were mistaken. She knew her birthday, and she didn't see Akita on or after her birthday.

When asked how she celebrated her birthday, Diana stated that she worked that day and then stopped at a store to get something out of layaway. No mention of gifts, a cake, or a special meal.

Diana Ervin told police that France never touched Akita. She did not believe the stories about him being inappropriate with her child.

Police asked Diana about the insurance policy her mother had on Akita's life.

Diana said all the money went to the funeral home. Marjorie Smith, Akita's grandmother, told police days earlier that Diana had come to her home asking for money; she wanted a few dollars from the policy. Smith told her no, and the two argued. Diane said this wasn't true; she'd asked her mother for $800 to purchase a plot where Akita would be buried.

Police then asked if there was ever any fighting between her and her daughter. Diana said no, there was never any violence. She'd never struck her child, nothing worse than a push. She did grab Akita's arm once, to stop her from leaving. Diana looked at the officer and asked, "Are all your leads leading back to me?"

Then she was asked about Gary France and his relationship with Akita. Had he ever struck her or her daughter? She said no; she denied that France ever tried to run her, Diana, down with his car. Diana did tell the officer that she attacked France after Akita was found, telling him that if he did anything to Akita, she was gone and she would leave.

They asked if she was an alcoholic, and Diana said no. Did she ever black out while drinking? Again, no. Did she clean Akita's room after Akita disappeared? No. They asked if she had mental health issues or ever received psychiatric treatment. She told them that she had mood swings but that she wasn't homicidal or suicidal.

Diana Ervin agreed to take a polygraph. Before the polygraph commenced, she had several questions for the officers. Was Akita's body far from the road? Was she covered with brush? Was it a bloody scene?

The officer reminded her that they were still waiting on a report from the medical examiner. Even if this officer had seen Akita's body when it was discovered, he wouldn't have shared that information with Diana Ervin.

At the end of July, police interviewed Diana's mother, Marjorie Smith. They talked about the last time she saw Akita. Smith told police that Diana and Akita drove to her house and the three of them got in her car to go to the Kroger in Commerce Township for groceries. Diana Ervin also mentioned this trip in her interview with the police. Smith drove because she had the largest trunk and could transport more food.

Usually, Smith wrote a check for her groceries, but on this day, she paid cash and had thrown away the sales slip. She thought they went shopping on the ninth or tenth of June. After shopping, they went to Diana's home to drop off groceries and then returned to Smith's house. Diana and Akita then visited for an hour or so. Akita and Diana left, but Smith was certain she saw Akita again, either that night or the next. She didn't think it was June 10 because Diana worked that day, but again, she wasn't certain.

Diana told her mother that she went to work on the tenth and called her on the eleventh to let her know Akita was missing. Marjorie Smith did not see Diana on her birthday.

Now that Smith considered it, Diana didn't take any time off work after Akita went missing. She worked her primary job during the week and at her second job on the weekend.

Police asked Smith if Akita ever talked with her about problems at home with Diana and France.

No.

Had Akita talked about feeling unsafe?

No.

Was she aware of Akita drinking and smoking marijuana?

Yes, she was.

Did Diana and Akita get along?

Oh, yes. Maybe Diana got on her nerves a little.

Had Akita ever seen a psychiatrist?

No, but she thought Akita might have met with a counselor through Friend of the Court. She didn't think that the counselor was helpful to her grandchild.

Akita's headstone at the Oak Hill Cemetery in Pontiac. *Author's collection.*

They asked Smith if she liked Gary France, her daughter's live-in boyfriend. No, she didn't, and she didn't understand why Diana liked him either.

Marjorie Smith related a story to the officer about the family being at her house after Akita's funeral. She had a modest policy on Akita, just $2,000, and everyone wanted that money even though the policy wasn't enough to pay for the funeral or the custom heart-shaped grave marker for Akita's final resting place.

Smith became emotional about her grandchild. She told the officer that she was closer to Akita than anyone else. She'd been having Akita over to her house since she was six months old. She told them she often wondered: "Instead of killing her, why didn't they pack her up and bring her here?"

Marjorie Smith told police that she would help them find who killed Akita—even if it was someone that she knew.

When asked who she thought murdered Akita Ervin, Smith responded without hesitation: Gary France.

What if Akita's death was an accident? What if she died accidentally and her body was left in the woods?

Smith didn't know. She did know that France had a bad temper and blamed Akita for his relationship issues with Diana.

When asked if Smith had thrown away any of Akita's belongings, she said no. They asked if any of Akita's personal effects were gone from her room at Diana's home, and she said she didn't think so. She didn't think Diana would part with any of Akita's things. Then Smith pointed out that France was home alone while Diana worked; he could have disposed of things without anyone knowing.

On August 21, 1992, White Lake Police interviewed Sherry and Lynette Hall*. The Hall family lived in the same neighborhood as Akita, and the girls were good friends, with Akita frequently coming to their home up until January 1992. Lynette told police that while Akita had boyfriends, some in Pontiac, some by her grandma's house, she wasn't aware of any who had been to her home in White Lake.

Lynette and Sherry both confirmed that Akita didn't like her mother's boyfriend and that she told them that he had touched her inappropriately. Sherry, Lynette's mother, said that Diana and France fought about Akita and that France didn't like it when Diana spent money on Akita. Lynette said that when she spent the night at Akita's house, the girls stayed in her room until France went to bed; only then did they come out.

On September 2, 1992, two White Lake detectives arrived at the home of Gary France, the trailer he'd shared with Diana and Akita Ervin. They confronted France with allegations of inappropriate contact with Akita, which he denied. They told him they knew he'd offered Akita, a fifteen-year-old girl, marijuana, cocaine, and liquor. France also denied these accusations; he asserted that he'd never touched Akita. He stated that he had never offered her liquor or marijuana, but some of his was missing and he suspected that she'd taken it. He said he didn't hurt Akita; he didn't kill her.

Investigators invited him to take a polygraph, but France said he'd have to think about it. He said he would tell them the next day what he decided. When the police didn't hear back from him within forty-eight hours, they returned to his home. France said he had already taken and passed a polygraph; he wasn't taking another one. He said the police couldn't charge him with anything. He wanted them to leave.

On October 1, 1992, police ran down the names of some of Akita's supposed boyfriends, names that had come up during the investigation: young men she "ran the streets" with in Pontiac. Mick Martinson and Jerry Arron* were both incarcerated and in custody the week that Akita was murdered. Another young man she was tied to, with a street name of Boo, was also in jail when Akita disappeared.

The first week of December, a neighbor of Diana Ervin and Gary France appeared at the White Lake Police Station. He said he had information about the case. Ken Hillard* told police that he had lived near Gary France for several years, and in that time, he had never known France to go fishing. France never had fishing gear and never talked about fishing.

However, the week that Akita disappeared, France suddenly had a rod and reel, as well as a tackle box. Hillard saw France leaving the house with these items.

He spoke to France a few weeks later, perhaps in late July or early August, and France told Hillard, "I go fishing there all the time!" Hillard claimed this statement wasn't true and shared with police that France was a mean and violent drunk, something he'd seen time and again in the years they'd been neighbors.

Hillard also told police that the day before Akita vanished, he found her washing France's car in the morning. France was standing nearby, supervising. He told Hillard that he was paying Akita three bucks to wash the car. As Hillard left for work, France went back to ordering Akita around, pointing out areas that she'd missed.

At the station, Diana told police that she saw Akita on June 10, around nine o'clock at night, when she, Diana, was leaving for work. When she returned home the next morning, she didn't check Akita's room but went directly to bed. When she woke up around one o'clock in the afternoon, she opened Akita's bedroom door, but the girl was gone. She did notice that Akita's ashtray was empty, which she found unusual. Akita smoked cigarettes, and she identified the brand of cigarettes to the police.

When police spoke to Gary France, he told them that after Diana left for work the evening of the tenth, he and Akita watched TV until one in the morning. He said Akita made a phone call around midnight, but he didn't think she received any calls. He volunteered to police that Akita used to run with crackheads in Pontiac. France said that he and Akita didn't always get along, but they were getting along that night. He described Akita as being in a good mood.

After speaking with Akita's mother and her live-in boyfriend, the police obtained a search warrant for the mobile home.

When they served the warrant, they spoke with Diana Ervin as they searched. She volunteered that Akita owed money to a dope man in Pontiac—at least, that's what she heard from Akita's father. She offered them a name but said she didn't know how much money Akita owed.

Police asked Diana Ervin and Gary France to come to the Michigan State Police post to take a polygraph exam. Both of them agreed. At the station, the couple paused outside of the building to smoke. When they tossed their butts on the ground, the police made a note of the brand. Perhaps they hoped to connect them with cigarette butts found near Akita's body when she was recovered.

Police searched their vehicles and the car belonging to Marjorie Smith. The bedding from Akita's room was collected and examined. Whatever evidence they collected did not add up to enough to identify a suspect or to make an arrest.

While police spent months investigating Akita's death, no one was ever arrested, charged, or named a person of interest. With little to go on, her case went cold.

It's hard to find mention of Akita's case these days. There are a few links online, classmates, family, and friends who remember the pretty dark-haired girl. Akita's case remains open, and White Lake Police are accepting tips and leads.

Akita's mother, Diana Ervin, passed away in early 2019. Gary France has also passed on. Akita's father, siblings, and cousins are still hoping for answers.

2
PAUL GIRARD
1988

With a population of twenty-one thousand, Marquette is the largest city in Michigan's upper peninsula, and the population has mostly stayed the same since 1988, when our story is set. Marquette is a college town, home to Northern Michigan University, and when the students arrive in the fall, the city's population climbs by several thousand.

One of the popular destinations in Marquette, which is the name of both the city and the county it sits in, is Presque Isle Park. Presque Isle translates to "almost island." Presque Isle Park is a 323-acre park on a peninsula that juts north into Lake Superior.

It was originally used as a lighthouse station to guide ships through the Great Lakes. There is a road from the city of Marquette into the park, and today the park has picnic areas, hiking trails, playgrounds, a band shell, and fields. There are several good places for fishing as well.

The park is home to rare albino deer and dozens of other animal species. It's a great place to observe and connect with nature. There's also a large marina and, of course, the Upper Harbor lighthouse. While Marquette is the largest community in the upper peninsula, it's still a small town, and in 1988, it wasn't too different from other small towns in the way that its residents viewed outsiders, which includes those who are different.

Our victim, Paul Girard, was known in the community as an openly gay man, and he was sometimes discriminated against because of it.

Girard's neighbors complained that people left his house at odd hours, and sometimes locals harassed him by calling him names or shouting insults

in his direction or at his modest residence on Division Street. Girard didn't let the harassment get to him and went on about his business, working, spending time with his friends, and remaining close to his family.

Paul Girard was one of three children. He had two sisters, Sue and Mary. He grew up in a Catholic family. The Girard home was a small farm where they kept some livestock and a garden to provide extra food for the dinner table. From a young age, Paul worked with his dad at a sawmill on the property and had a knack for fixing things. His sisters fondly recall their brother was affectionate, generous, and kind.

Paul worked at a rental shop repairing small engines. The money he made at the shop wasn't a fabulous income, but he got by.

In late September 1988, classes were in session at Northern Michigan University. Girard was known to pick up men from the university at local bars and take them somewhere more private. In 1988, discretion was important.

Around three o'clock in the morning on September 30, Paul Girard was spotted at a gas station on the city's south end. He was last seen by himself getting into his blue Honda. This was the last time he was seen alive. Paul Girard was murdered at approximately four o'clock in the morning on September 30.

Opposite: Presque Isle Park. *Ashley Trowbridge.*

Above: Chief Kawbawgam's grave site. The body of Paul Girard was found nearby. *Ashley Trowbridge.*

His body was discovered around ten in the morning by two people out for a walk. According to an AP report, the thirty-four-year-old had been stabbed forty times, and his throat was slashed.

Girard's body was found just a few feet away from the large stone marking Chief Kawbawgam's grave site. Near his body, police found his glasses and a folding knife.

It appears that there was a struggle, and Paul went for his knife to defend himself, but he didn't have a chance to open it and fight back. They found his light-blue Honda parked in a lot not far from where he was found. Missing from the bloody scene were his wallet and car keys, but robbery was never thought to be a motive for the attack. According to a 2020 story in the *Mining Journal*, the murder weapon was never recovered.

On October 1, 1988, Paul's death was the top story in the local paper, and the front page shouted, "Gay Community Shocked by Murder." The headline was the attention grabber. Locals were buzzing with speculation about the crime. Some thought he propositioned the wrong man, while others thought maybe a couple of locals cornered him and did him in.

Girard's brutal murder led to a huge response from local law enforcement. This was the first murder in Marquette since 1985, and police recognized it as a hate crime. Someone had targeted Girard because he was a gay man. In 1988, hate crime legislation was not yet in existence. The Hate Crimes Statistics Act did not become law until April 1990, when President George Herbert Walker Bush signed off on it.

Marquette Police Detective Mike Angeli said Girard was well known to police because of his gay lifestyle. He was often victimized by those who opposed the way he lived.

Every detective in Marquette worked on the case. The entire month of October was spent running down leads and processing evidence from the scene, and police had a lot to process, including fingerprints, footprints, fibers, and blood evidence.

Lower-priority crimes like bad checks and break-ins were pushed aside. This case was the top priority and focus for Marquette PD.

Detective Salvatore Sarvello told the local paper, the *Mining Journal*, that police were working with assistance from the state police crime lab in Marquette. The Federal Bureau of Investigation was called in, although the agency declined to specify what kind of support the FBI was providing. Experts from the University of Michigan downstate in Ann Arbor were also consulted.

On October 12, 1988, police released a description of their suspect: a white male, twenty to twenty-five years old, with dark curly hair and a full mustache. He was wearing a dark jacket and tan pants on the night of the murder. Someone matching this description was seen on foot leaving the park around four thirty that morning.

By the end of October, a $2,000 reward had been posted for information leading to the arrest of the person responsible for Girard's brutal slaying. Detective Salvatore Sarvello and fellow Detective Hank Steed were heading up the investigation in November 1988.

They told the *Mining Journal* they felt tremendous pressure to find the perpetrator. Investigators spoke of their frustration at receiving misleading information about the case.

Marquette is a college town, and thousands of students arrive each fall and stay through the long, snowy winter; "unsolved murder" was not what the families of students wanted to hear. The detectives worked on the case under unrelenting pressure.

As of this writing, Girard's case is the largest investigation ever undertaken by the Marquette Police Department. Unfortunately, it wasn't enough. Girard's killer was never named or arrested. In January 1989, three months after Girard's murder, police downstate in Kalamazoo shared information on a similar slaying that occurred within days of the Presque Isle murder—a stabbing of an openly gay man. A brief story in the *Battle Creek Enquirer* outlined similarities between the cases.

The victim in Kalamazoo received over one hundred stab wounds. Investigating agencies compared notes and ruled out a connection between the murders. In April 1989, police received a tip leading them to a local man to interview about Girard's murder. The interview was promising, and the local man became the primary suspect. Unfortunately, there was no evidence connecting him to the crime scene, and the *Mining Journal* identified him only as someone who lived and worked in Marquette County.

In May 1989, both Marquette Mayor Robert Berube and Police Chief George Johnson weighed in. They knew that police had a suspect, and Berube cautioned locals not to speculate or spread rumors. Chief Johnson was quoted as saying that the department would continue to investigate the case and follow up on tips as they came in.

In July 1989, there was another article in the paper. This time, the Detroit-based Michigan lesbian-gay Anti-Violence Project was decrying Girard's murder. Representatives pointed out that gays and lesbians are often subject to violence that isn't reported, and if it is reported, it's not properly investigated.

A spokesman for the group, Mark Loveless, said he couldn't single out the Marquette force specifically because he wasn't familiar with their investigation. A detective responded to his comment by saying that he agreed Girard's lifestyle led to his death, but it did not affect the way Marquette police investigated his case.

Months passed, and then years—the Girard case went cold.

It wasn't forgotten. A town like Marquette doesn't see enough violent crime to make a case like this fade from memory. Girard's killer was clever enough or, more likely, lucky enough not to leave evidence behind that would lead back to him.

Every few years, the case appears in the paper again. In 2008, on the twentieth anniversary of his death, the *Mining Journal* published another story. Reporters interviewed Salvatore Sarvello, one of the lead detectives on the case. Eventually, he was promoted to police chief, but by 2008, he had retired.

Sarvello addressed one of the big issues of the case: the setting of the murder, in the early morning hours in a public park off one of the Great Lakes. It's not the ideal setting for preserving evidence, nor were there witnesses around to report what they saw.

In the published interview, Sarvello noted that Marquette has only two unsolved murders: Paul Girard from 1988 and the 2000 murder of Erin Taylor.

In the decades since Paul Girard died in a college town in northern Michigan, many things have changed. His parents passed on: his father in 1994 and his mother in 2005. The Marquette Police Department has seen many changes. Mike Angeli went from detective to police chief and later to city manager, and in 2021, he retired.

George Johnson, who was chief of police in 1988, passed away. Salvatore Sarvello, who led the investigation along with Hank Steed, has since passed away.

Something that hasn't changed since Girard's death is the phone number of the Marquette Police Department: 906-228-0400. If you have information about the murder of Paul Girard, contact the detective bureau.

3

MATTHEW LEACH

1992

Friday, July 24, 1992, was a typical summer day in Michigan. The temperature was in the high seventies. Twenty-two-year-old Matthew Leach had plans that night: He was going to see a former girlfriend.

Matthew was finally looking to the future. He'd run into some legal issues a year or two earlier and spent time in jail for drunk driving. Matthew went from jail to a transition house and then moved in with one of his brothers.

Matthew came from a big family. His parents, Herb Sr. and Janette, had five children: Herb Jr., Jeff, Chris, Matt, and Kathy. In the summer of 1992, Matthew was living with his brother Jeff.

On this summer evening, Matthew is getting ready to meet up with his former girlfriend. Matthew wanted to look good for their meeting, to show her he's still got it.

Jeff's girlfriend April* helped Matthew adjust his necklace, which had a distinctive eagle pendant. Matthew left his brother's house wearing black boots with metal trim, designer jeans, and a "Joe Cool" Camel cigarette brand T-shirt.

It's hard to call the meeting with the former girlfriend a date; they wanted to sit down and talk. The two planned to discuss their current relationships, their feelings, and where things stood between them.

It was just after ten o'clock when Louise Kinney* picked Matthew up at Jeff's house. This was the last time Jeff and April saw Matthew.

The now-closed Coney Island where Matthew Leach met with his former girlfriend before he was murdered. *Author's collection.*

Louise and Matthew drove to Colonial Coney Island on Corunna Road in Flint, less than a mile from Jeff's house.

Louise was frustrated by Matthew during their time in the restaurant. She could tell that he had a couple of drinks, and it appeared he might have been under the influence of marijuana. The two of them returned to Louise's car to continue the conversation, but things quickly devolved into an argument.

Matthew was critical of Louise's new boyfriend and made some unkind remarks. The fight escalated verbally, and Matthew exited her vehicle.

Louise opened the window and called Matthew to come back, hoping they could finish their conversation, but according to Louise, Matthew ignored her and began walking westbound on Corunna Road.

Louise started her car and drove away, heading for her boyfriend's house.

When Matthew hadn't returned to his brother's home by Sunday afternoon, calls were made, and Matthew's siblings and parents realized that no one had seen Matthew or spoken to him.

Matthew's father, Herb Leach Sr., filed a missing person's report with the police in Flint.

On Friday, July 31, 1992, two locals decided to take a walk in the woods not far from M 21, and they headed down South Reed Road, not far from the old quarry.

As they entered the edge of the woods, they noticed a terrible smell and thought that there must be a dead deer nearby. Following the odor, they came across human remains. The remains were face down, clad only in underpants. A mass of dark curly hair was visible across the head and neck.

The two locals quickly retreated and drove to a nearby pay phone, summoning the police.

The sheriff's department responded to the scene and placed a call to the Michigan State Police crime lab, asking for assistance in a homicide.

None of Matthew's belongings were at the scene. His jewelry and effects, including that distinctive eagle pendant and his fancy black leather boots, were missing.

Matthew's remains were transported to Sparrow Hospital in Lansing for an autopsy. The body was not in good shape. After a full week outdoors in the summer, the heat had sped up decomposition.

Animal and insect activity also took their toll. Matthew was identified via X-ray, and his cause of death was listed as blunt force trauma.

In a heart-wrenching aside, Herb Sr. was in his car listening to the radio while driving to Alma, Michigan, for a Shriners' event. That's when he heard a news report of a body being found near Corunna. Herb pulled into the Shiawassee County State Police post and inquired about the body. He told them that his boy was missing.

The police shared what they knew, which wasn't much this early in the investigation. They directed him to the sheriff's department. The next day, Herb Leach Sr. received the call confirming his worst fears. The body found in the woods was his son Matthew.

The Shiawassee County sheriff immediately started looking for suspects. They spoke with Matthew's parents and interviewed his brothers.

During an interview with Jeff, with whom Matthew was living, Jeff said that before he left to see Louise, Matthew gave Jeff money to buy beer. Jeff assumed that Matthew was coming home after he met with Louise Kinney. When Matthew didn't come home, Jeff assumed their meeting went well and his brother was with Louise.

Louise Kinney and her boyfriend were interviewed, and she relayed the story that you read earlier. The two of them went to Colonial Coney Island and started talking. Then they moved the conversation out to the car. The two of them argued, and Matthew exited the vehicle. He was headed west on Corunna Road, and she tried to get him back into the car, but he refused. She then drove to her boyfriend's place and spent the night with him.

Louise Kinney was issued a polygraph examination, but the results were inconclusive.

Police also interviewed another woman Matthew was seeing at the time. She lived about fifteen miles away in Byron, Michigan, but was not considered a suspect in Matthew's case.

In September 1992, sheriff's department investigators were working on the case, and in the hopes of ruling out some of the people closest to Matthew, they began issuing polygraphs. Matthew's brothers were issued polygraphs. His brothers either passed the polygraph or the results were inconclusive. This was a frustrating set of developments, as they wanted a suspect to zero in on.

Sadly, between 1992 and 1993, no arrests were made, and the murder of Matthew Leach went cold. His case was reinvestigated in the late 1990s without any progress.

With the thirtieth anniversary of his murder approaching, his case was reviewed again, this time under the direction of Shiawassee County Sheriff Douglass Chapman. Chapman reached out to Mark Pendergraff, a former Michigan State Police detective.

Pendergraff is well respected in law enforcement circles, perhaps best known for his work on the 1973 murder of Dawn Magyar.

Magyar, a young mother who was last seen in Owosso on January 27, 1973, left behind a one-year-old son. Her body was found on March 4, 1973.

After a multiyear investigation, her killer, Jerald Wingeart, was arrested in March 2001 and eventually sentenced to life in prison. Wingeart died in prison back in 2022.

Pendergraff, who has decades of experience in law enforcement, wasn't put off by the age of the case. He dug in and performed a review of the voluminous case file. Pendergraff was quick to point out that the sheriff's department did good work on the case over the years, but he intended to start at square one and revisit all the evidence.

Pendergraff interviewed hundreds of people, most of whom were interviewed in the 1990s, to see if their recollections had changed or improved with time. He also reissued polygraphs to witnesses and suspects, attempting to glean new insight into the case.

Pendergraff is incredibly knowledgeable about the Leach case, studying it from every angle and running down each lead.

While Pendergraff did a deep dive into the file, no one was arrested or charged in Matthew's murder.

One of the peculiar things about this case is that Matthew Leach was found wearing only his underwear. Could he have been caught in a compromising situation that led to his death? Perhaps after leaving Louise, he met up with another girl and things got out of hand.

Matthew's clothing, including his fancy boots, has never been recovered. If someone took him to that isolated location to kill him, would they make him strip to his undies, kill him, and take his clothing away? That seems unlikely.

It's possible he was caught somewhere in a state of undress, assaulted, and then his body was transported and dumped in the woods. Maybe being in only his underwear is just a weird fact of the case. But it could point to the motive for his murder.

Matthew has siblings who are hoping for justice, and his father, Herb Sr., is still alive and looking for answers.

While the murder of Matthew Leach was thoroughly investigated and revisited in 2022, it remains open and unsolved. If you have information about the murder of Matthew Leach, please contact the Shiawassee County Sheriff's Office at 989-743-3411.

4

VALERIE BISHOP

1977

In February 1977, Valerie Bishop was ten years old. She was one of six children and a fourth grader at Carver Elementary School in Detroit. Valerie came from a big family. She had two older brothers, one younger sister, and two younger brothers. Their mother, Ida Bishop, had moved the family up from Alabama a few years earlier. There were jobs in Detroit—opportunity. Ida Bishop wanted her children to have options to be successful, so they moved into the house on Aurora near the intersection of Wyoming and Plymouth on Detroit's west side.

On February 2, Valerie was outside playing after school. It was a warm day for February in Michigan with temperatures in the mid-thirties, and Valerie and her siblings were playing outside with friends.

Her mother was looking for one of the boys, one of Valerie's older brothers, to head up to the corner store—Houston's party store—and pick up a gallon of milk. When she couldn't find one of the boys, she asked Valerie to run the errand for her.

Valerie was supposed to walk with one of her friends, but she ended up walking alone—a trip she'd made a dozen times before. The store's owner, Sam Houston, later told the police Valerie did come in and purchase milk, and nothing seemed out of the ordinary.

Valerie did not return home right away. At first, Ida wasn't worried. Kids lose track of time. She located her older boys and told them to find their sister and bring her home. When they couldn't locate Valerie, Mrs. Bishop called the Detroit Police Department, telling them that her oldest daughter was missing. Detroit police came out right away. They took a missing child report from Ida Bishop.

According to Valerie's sister, Kimberly, "They called Detroit police. It became apparent that something had happened because it seemed like everything started moving so fast after that, then the police came and that right there started it all. It all started after the police showed up. They took it seriously because she was a little girl."

February in Michigan, it gets dark early. At seven o'clock at night, when Detroit police took the report, it was fully dark, making it hard to perform a proper search for the missing fourth grader.

Police went door to door that evening, canvassing the neighborhood, asking if anyone had seen Valerie or seen anything suspicious.

In the morning, the search resumed, and officers checked out a vacant house less than a block away from the Bishop home.

At the empty house, the police made a grim discovery. They saw blood spattered along the side of the garage, and when officers dug around in the snow, they found Valerie's body still dressed for the winter weather—athletic shoes, red socks, a red dress, a winter jacket, and gloves. The milk she'd purchased at Houston's party store was on the ground nearby.

The blood spatter they saw on the garage likely came from the impact wound on the side of Valerie's head, not from the multiple stab wounds in her abdomen.

The vacant garage that Valerie was found next to is located off an alleyway, Valerie was left on the side of the road, covered with snow, just waiting to be found. Valerie was not a big girl, according to her autopsy; she was four feet, eight inches tall and weighed just seventy-four pounds.

That afternoon, Detroit police came to tell Ida Bishop they'd found her daughter.

Reflecting on that terrible moment, Valerie's younger sister, Kimberly, said, "She (Mother Ida) sent us all into the back room and we all went to the back room. When they told her, she just let out a scream that you'll never forget."

While the Bishop family grieved the unimaginable loss of sweet Valerie, the community rallied around them. Family, friends, and neighbors brought dishes of hot food or visited to pay their respects.

Kimberly recalled, "It was a lot of people, just a lot of people coming and trying to comfort my mom. The people in the neighborhood came and just a lot of people, and the news was there. I remember our principals from the school coming to the house. I just remember a lot of people."

These same neighbors were cooperative and helpful with the investigation. This cooperation led police to a suspect in the case, thirty-year-old Moses Potter, a Black man who lived in the neighborhood. Kimberly Bishop pointed out that Potter was a former Detroit police officer.

Valerie's body was recovered from the back of an abandoned house on Cedarlawn, almost directly behind the duplex where Moses Potter lived. According to a story in the *Detroit Free Press*, Potter had an interesting history. At the time of Valerie's murder, he was a student at Wayne State University. He was also unemployed and recently split from his wife.

According to a February 8, 1977 story in the *Detroit Free Press*, Potter signed up with the Detroit Police Department in 1970 and went through the academy. Then he took a position with the Eleventh Precinct. His time with the department did not go well.

Rather than hiring him at the end of his probationary period, it was recommended that his probation be extended for six months. Potter didn't have a good reputation and struggled to find officers who wanted to partner with him. He was also transferred from the Eleventh Precinct to the Tenth Precinct in the hope that it would improve his situation.

Potter complained that his supervisors were pressuring him unfairly and not letting him succeed.

At the end of this six-month extension, Potter was set to be terminated and the department advised him to seek psychiatric help.

However, rather than allow himself to be fired, he skipped his scheduled probationary meeting and then submitted his resignation from the department. This happened almost five years to the day before Valerie's murder on February 2, 1972.

Potter had no criminal record and was reportedly doing satisfactory work in his courses at Wayne State. On Friday, February 4, just days after Valerie's murder, Moses Potter was arrested and held pending a preliminary hearing later in the month.

Among the items collected during his arrest were a pair of light-blue pants with visible bloodstains on them.

A witness from the neighborhood told police that she saw a broad-shouldered, bald African American man wearing light-blue pants standing in the alley and watching a young girl. While Potter was not bald, he did have a receding hairline and broad shoulders.

The pants collected from his home matched the description of what the man in the alley was wearing, and those pants had blood on them.

When the lab tested Potter's pants using the finest technology available at the start of 1977, they found that the blood was O positive, the same type as Valerie Bishop. But this is also the most common blood type, a factor the judge had to consider.

Another piece of evidence brought up at the hearing was a brown hair found on Valerie's clothing; this piece of hair was six inches in length. The hair did not belong to Valerie or Moses Potter.

The hair is an intriguing piece of evidence, but we don't know where on Valerie it was found. If it was on her dress or coat, it could have come from a classmate at school, a friend in the neighborhood, or even from one of her teachers.

Valerie suffered a terrible fate. From autopsy reports, it appears that someone struck her in the side of the head, perhaps using a board or a brick, and she was likely hit more than once.

Then her killer attempted a sexual assault. His monstrous work wasn't done. Valerie was stabbed three times in the abdomen and her body hastily covered with snow.

It is painful to know that she was murdered in such a violent and cruel way. The bright shining light of the Bishop family. Ida Bishop's oldest daughter died alone in an alleyway on a February night.

In the days after Valerie was laid to rest, the Bishop house fell silent. The visits ended, the hot dishes stopped arriving, and the family was wrapped up in missing their girl.

Kimberly said, "I guess the last thing a mother can hear when their child is being hurt or think of that their child may think of them as a mother, mothers comfort their children. Maybe she just felt like she wasn't there to help her. I don't know, but it just, the house was silent. It was so much sadness, so much grief."

On February 12, Lieutenant Isaiah "Ike" McKinnon, head of the Sex Crimes Unit for Detroit police, was interviewed by the *Michigan Chronicle* newspaper. McKinnon told readers, "We as adults must look out for all children, not just our own. What we're realistically talking about is taking care of one another."

When asked, McKinnon said that he remembered seeing Potter around the Tenth Precinct back in 1971, but he didn't know him particularly well. If McKinnon's name sounds familiar, he went on to become the chief of police in Detroit and serve the city as deputy mayor.

Now in his eighties, McKinnon is retired but still appears at public functions. Ike McKinnon, like Valerie Bishop, was born in Alabama and came north for better opportunities.

Her case was worked by Detroit police, led by homicide investigator Robert Hislop. With Potter in custody, it appeared they had their man.

During the week of February 14, Moses Potter appeared before visiting recorders court Judge William J. Sutherland. Evidence was presented, including eyewitness testimony from the woman who saw a broad-shouldered, bald African American man in the alley watching a young girl.

Additional evidence included the blood on Potter's pants, the same type as Valerie's, but the same type as many people. The hair, a six-inch-long light-brown hair found on Valerie's clothing, was also presented as hair that did not belong to Valerie Bishop or Moses Potter.

On Monday, February 21, Sutherland found that the prosecution failed to prove their case against Potter, and he dismissed the charges without prejudice. This meant that if more evidence came to light, Potter could again be charged.

According to a February 22, 1977 story in the *Detroit Free Press*, Judge Sutherland told the court that he did a lot of soul searching over the weekend. While he was a father with young children of his own, he had to dismiss the case for lack of evidence.

A spokesman from the Wayne County Prosecutor's Office said they planned to appeal Sutherland's decision, but nothing ever came of it. Potter went on about his life, and the Bishop family continued without Valerie.

Kimberly Bishop described the time after the dismissal: "Without her, it was time for us to grow up. After that, we knew that this was going to be a tough world. We had to prepare ourselves. My mother became so overprotective she wouldn't let me go anywhere with my friends or anything. She was just really protective of me, which made me rebel. Of course, I eventually settled down and realized that my mother was one of the strongest women I knew, so I too had to be strong."

There is some good news in this still unsolved case. According to the records department of the Detroit Police Department, Valerie's files still exist and appear to be intact.

The Wayne County Coroner's Office still has her autopsy report. There is continued hope that a cold case unit of the Detroit police will take another look at her case. There is also hope that the pants that Moses Potter was wearing, light-blue pants with bloodstains, perhaps too are in evidence.

Valerie's case deserves a second look. If the biological materials, including the hair found on her clothing, are still available and can be tested, what story could that evidence tell us?

Valerie's mother, Ida, and her siblings are still around, and some live in the Detroit area. Ida Bishop didn't move away from the Aurora Street house that Valerie once called home until a couple of years ago.

Her family is still waiting and still wondering what happened to their little girl. If you have information on the 1977 murder of Valerie Bishop, please contact the Detroit Police Department.

> *I want to see her case come back into the community. I want people to realize that she was somebody's daughter and sister. She was somebody's friend. She was always a good helper, always someone good to talk to. She was absolutely beautiful. She was strong, she was courageous, she was my everything. She was my hero. She was everything to me.*
>
> —*Kimberly Bishop*

5

GREGORY McROBERTS

1991

In December 1991, just a couple of weeks before Christmas, Gregory McRoberts was spending time with his fiancée, Amy, and their daughter, Teigha, preparing for the holidays.

Amy and Greg had begun dating just two years earlier when she was nineteen years old. Greg's fiancée was pregnant with their second child, and Amy fondly remembers the last day she had with Greg.

She said that Greg was in good spirits; the couple spent the morning Christmas shopping, and while they were struggling financially, the two were young and in love. The future seemed bright with promise.

On that mild December Thursday, Greg was listening to music, a song by Ozzy Osbourne, or perhaps a track from Ozzy's band, Black Sabbath. He was into the music and telling Amy about it, asking her to listen to the lyrics, the rhythm. He was cheerful and upbeat.

According to police records, it was a bit after five o'clock, Greg left the home in Amy's car; he needed to buy cigarettes and make a phone call. The trailer the family called home did not have a phone line, and this was a few years before the advent of cellular technology. While he was out, the car broke down. Greg was good with his hands and knew he could fix the vehicle, so he returned home on foot, told Amy what happened, and said he would fix the car. Greg collected some tools and left again, this time on his bicycle.

Greg did not have a car of his own; he used Amy's vehicle, or more frequently, he used his bicycle to get around town. Greg was known to ride his bike all over, even in cold weather. He used the bike to get to and from work at the local Big Lots store.

At the end of 1991, Greg McRoberts worked hard to get himself together. Like many guys in their early twenties, he'd made some missteps along the way. He knew it was time to get right and plan for his future and the future of his young family. It wasn't just him anymore; there were other people to consider.

Greg and Amy had a daughter and were expecting a second child in the spring of 1992. While they were going through what some might call a lean period, Greg was dedicated to Amy and their daughter, Teigha. He confided in his friends at work that he was excited about the arrival of a second child. He loved his family, and Greg wanted to do right by them, to be the best partner, the best father, the best man that he could be for those who counted on him.

Greg's own family was a good example of love, support, and hard work. His parents, Richard and Deanna, had recently celebrated their twenty-fifth wedding anniversary. They had a happy marriage that produced four children: Pamela, Thomas, Mark, and Greg. The McRobertses worked hard; his dad worked at the local service station, and in addition to keeping the home and raising four children, his mom worked at a restaurant.

When the car broke down, it was late in the afternoon on Thursday. Greg walked home, collected the tools he needed for the repair, and headed out again, this time on his bike. By the time he got on the road and made it back to the car, it was fully dark. December in Michigan, the sun sets early.

While Greg returned to the disabled vehicle, Amy waited for him. Their young daughter, Teigha, toddled about the house, waiting for Daddy to come back. Amy was hoping the baby would stay up long enough for Greg to kiss her good night, but when he wasn't back in time, she changed the baby into pajamas and tucked her in her crib.

Since their home was without a phone, Amy couldn't call anyone to check on Greg or offer him a hand. She may have figured that the car repair was taking longer than expected. Eventually, she fell asleep. When Amy woke up, it was after eleven o'clock, and Greg wasn't back. She was worried—what if he was stuck? What if he'd gone to the bar? Amy dressed the baby and slipped on a warm coat; there was snow on the ground, and it was dark and cold out.

Amy stepped outside and headed for the road; she intended to walk to the Silver Inn, where Greg told her the car was. As she reached Meridian Road, a chill came over her. She was frightened. Amy looked up the long, dark road, and then back toward her house. Her tiny daughter snuggled against her. She turned around and went back to their place. Amy didn't know where Greg was, but something told her it could wait until morning.

When the sun rose on Friday, December 13, 1991, there was no sign of Greg or his bike. The family car wasn't back; neither was her partner, Teigha's daddy. Perhaps Greg went to his parents' home or ran into a friend. Amy thought maybe he would return, but he didn't. She asked a neighbor if she could use their phone to call Greg's parents and see if he was there. The McRobertses had not seen or heard from their son.

On Monday, one of Greg's brothers filed a missing person's report with the Midland County sheriff. Law enforcement began a search for twenty-four-year-old Greg McRoberts.

Amy's car was located at the Silver Creek Inn, on South Meridian Road in Midland. There was no sign of Greg, and the repairs he intended to make were not complete. Greg's parents, siblings, and friends were all contacted. Had anyone seen him? The answer, time and again, was no.

At first, some thought Greg had run off, the responsibilities of home and family too much for a young guy. Amy didn't believe it; she thought back to the two of them spending time with their daughter, listening to music. How happy Greg seemed. He'd shown no sign of agitation or displeasure. He was excited about the arrival of their second child.

Greg's parents, Richard and Deanna, did not believe that he would abandon Amy or Teigha. They knew their son wasn't perfect, but for him to up and leave was completely out of character.

The days ticked by, one after the other. Greg's mom, Deanna, kept two bottles of Coca-Cola in the fridge, one for her and one for Greg. When her son stopped by for a visit, the two drank Cokes while they chatted; she knew that day would come again and wanted to be ready. But her heart was heavy with fear and worry about her blue-eyed, fair-haired son. Christmas Day arrived, and the family gathered to exchange gifts. There was no sign of Greg.

The new year arrived, full of promise, but it was gray and dark for those who loved and missed him. Greg's family and friends were still searching for him, tracing the route he must have taken on his bicycle that Thursday night.

Saturday, January 4, 1992, was unseasonably warm, with temperatures approaching fifty degrees. Of course, it was overcast and gray, and snow always threatened, but this day was different. Someone spotted something out of place in a ditch along Meridian Road. On closer examination, the something was someone. The body of a man lay next to a bicycle in the ditch by the road. Twenty-four-year-old Greg McRoberts—brother, son, father, and partner—was no longer missing.

The ditch along Meridian Road was between Greg's home and where his disabled car was left at the Silver Creek Inn. It appeared that Greg was fatally struck by a vehicle, sending him and his bike into the ditch.

The location of Greg's remains immediately raised red flags for his loved ones and the community. Meridian Road is a well-traveled route, particularly by those local to Midland. How could both his body and his bike have been there for nearly a month but no one saw or noticed anything?

At the time of his death, Greg's daughter was about sixteen months old, and his son wasn't yet born. Greg Jr., who goes by Scott, arrived later in 1992. His arrival was a blessing for the family, who missed Greg terribly, but difficult and unfair to the boy, who would never know his father or know how loved and wanted he was by his namesake.

Greg's family planned a funeral, and the community started whispering. A low rumble of rumors and speculation dominated the talk about Greg's case for decades.

After Greg's body was found, the rumor mill went into high gear. Word on the street was that Greg was targeted, that he was intentionally struck by a car. Perhaps as payback for some slight, something real or perceived. They said maybe someone followed Greg and hit him intentionally.

These rumors were hard to hear, but the next bit of speculation was worse.

People were saying that Greg wasn't killed in the accident. That his body and bike, left alongside Meridian Road, the same route they knew he would take from his home to the Silver Inn, where his car waited for repair, could not have been there for nearly a month without being seen. This area was searched in the days after the accident, and Greg wasn't there.

The talk was that the person who struck Greg must have stopped, loaded Greg's bike and his body into their vehicle, and transported him from the scene. Then they hid Greg's body for weeks, later returning his bike and his remains to the location where the accident occurred. One of the main rumors was fueled by the idea that Greg survived the accident and that the person or persons who struck him tried to nurse him back to health.

Since Greg was killed almost instantly, there was little substance to the rumors, but it didn't stop them from taking hold in the community. People were suspicious of one another: Could that be the person who hit Greg and then hid his body? Who would do that? Where was he held? Why return him to the site later? Was it guilt? Something else?

Speculation was rampant, and it was hurtful. The rumors not only harmed Greg's loved ones, who wondered why anyone would be so cruel as to conceal him, but also hindered the investigation into his death.

Police chased leads generated by the rumors, leads that took them nowhere but ate up time and resources. It was a frustrating situation and one that persisted for years. People called in tips about who held Greg after the accident, tips about bloodstained cars, suspicious pickup trucks, or abandoned barns. Police dutifully investigated each tip and ruled them out.

It's time to put this rumor to bed. Greg was killed almost instantly. Had the person who struck him or another passerby stopped to help Greg, they would have learned that he was dead, the impact knocking the life out of his young, healthy body. Even if the person who struck Greg stopped immediately and rendered aid, it would not have helped. The injuries Greg sustained in the accident were not compatible with life.

Greg's body wasn't removed from the scene. He was not taken to a private home or a barn or shed along with his bicycle; he died on December 12, 1991, and his body waited to be discovered, silently and patiently in a deep ditch along Meridian Road.

It was more than a decade before there was a real break in Greg's case. Something that kicked the investigation and the rumor mill into high gear once again.

The break came in 2005 in the form of a letter mailed to Greg's parents' home. A two-page letter neatly typed.

In many ways, this letter was meant as a gift for Greg's family. It was helpful to know what happened that night and how their son, partner, and father died. To know the circumstances of the accident. That there was a real person behind the crash that took Greg from them.

The letter read:

> *March 22, 2005*
> *To the family of Greg McRoberts,*
> *You do not know me, and I have never met you, but I need to confess something that has been heavy on my heart for a long time. I was driving the car that hit and killed Greg. I was traveling southbound on Meridian road. He was traveling north. I don't know why, but he was riding his bike in my lane. There are small wood guardrails there that are very close to the road. He may have thought I was farther away than I really was because I only had one headlight. Or maybe he was just not paying attention. I have no way of knowing. All I do know is that I didn't see him until it was too*

late. I tried to avoid him, but he slammed into the right passenger side of my vehicle. I panicked and fled. I know it was the wrong thing to do. I counted on the cars behind me stopping and helping him.

I did not stop, and did not know the outcome until a month later my neighbor told me that they had found him. That moment is etched on my memory and something inside of me also died knowing what had happened and the pain that I had caused. To leave a son, wife, and children alone is an unthinkably painful realization.

I am so sorry. Words cannot describe. I'll never forget that feeling, that hole it left in me. The guilt of my actions has many times brought me to desperation and crying in the years since that night. I just didn't want to believe that it happened. I have tried many ways to forget my actions and to drown my memory because then everything might be all right. I discovered that I couldn't take enough drugs or alcohol to cover the pain of my own guilt. But it just made me feel less worthwhile and made my own guilt worse. Hiding my actions has caused me to go into deep depression, an attempt to escape myself with alcohol and drugs and the loss of my marriage. In fact, they became a prison of my own making. Nothing worked, because no matter how hard I tried, you can't deny reality. In many ways, I wish I had turned myself in. I know that if I had turned myself in, I would have paid whatever price society would have deemed worthy and then maybe not have suffered with the guilt and shame through the years like I have.

In time I realized that I needed to make a change in my life. I started going through a 12-step program and getting in touch with my higher power. I ended up finding that higher power in a personal relationship with God. As I did that, I began to realize that I needed to deal with this one part of my life that I had for so long tried to forget. I needed to realize that the pain of the loss that I caused and the taking of his life doesn't leave me. I do not want to minimize in any way your pain over this loss you have suffered. I can only begin to imagine what you have had to go through in these years. It had to be even worse not knowing exactly what happened or who was responsible.

One time I was in Minnesota fishing with my brother. He was about 14 at the time. We were on a small island about 1 1/8 acres in size with a lot of steep rocks that went down into the water. All of a sudden he came up missing. I had this terrible gut-wrenching feeling that he had slipped into the water and went off the drop-off. I'll never forget that feeling, that hole it left in me. It brought me to desperation and crying and panic. That incident had haunted me because it was short-lived as I learned soon that he was all right. I cannot imagine having to live with something like that on an ongoing basis.

I have many times realized that you must have experienced that feeling over and over through the years.

Words cannot express how sorry I am. Writing this letter is a witness to this fact. I saw a lawyer a short time ago as I have tried to get my life back in order to turn myself in, and he advised me that the statute of limitations has passed and that I should just forget it and go on with my life. Somehow I just cannot do that. I have come to realize that to take his advice, to try and just forget, doesn't work, and to not care is to not free oneself to live. I feel like to be comfortable about just living and enjoying life as if nothing happened after you have taken a life is like living in contempt of that life. After much thought and counsel and prayer, I at least needed to do this one thing: to write you and confess to you and give you the circumstances of your son's death. I cannot give value to my life if I do not value the life of others, especially Greg's.

I'm making sure of one thing, though, because I'm alive and I know that I don't deserve it. I have made a commitment to God that I will seek to create and do as much good and help save as many lives as I can and make a positive impact on the world. I feel that I owe you and the world that. I have come to realize that time is so short and you have only so many opportunities. So I'm not just living for my life, I'm living for your son too, because he did matter and he still does matter greatly. In the last few years, I have come to realize that someone else has died because of me, Jesus Christ. My responsibility is to now live worthy of that incredible price.

I fear that this note will cause you much pain. That is not my hope. Saying that I am sorry seems too inadequate, yet I want to help us both bring some kind of closure to what was an unimaginable tragedy for you and a lifelong burden of guilt for me.

I know that nothing I can say or do can ever repay the life that was taken. I do want you to know that I refuse to take my actions lightly. I will live with the pain of my own actions for the rest of my life. I refuse to not accept responsibility for my actions. Please accept this letter as one of the steps that I am taking to make payment for my actions and to take responsibility for my past.

I pray for you almost daily. And I pray that you will find the peace that I am seeking and have begun to find in this confession. I do not know what

> *will come of this effort on my part. I fear that I have caused more pain rather than help for you. I cannot even begin to imagine that you will have anything but contempt for me. I didn't reveal this till now because I didn't want to reopen old wounds and cause you even more pain. But a friend of mine told me through experiences that it was really important for you to have some kind of closure on this. If this does cause you more pain, I am deeply sorry. I want to ask for your forgiveness, however, I also know that this might not be possible.*
>
> *If you need to respond to this confession on my part, good or bad, you may put an add* [sic] *in the personal section of the* Midland Daily News *from Greg's family.*

The letter didn't alleviate the rumors that somehow Greg survived the accident. Once again, people were saying Greg was taken from the scene by the letter writer, that Greg was concealed, his body hidden and later returned to the site.

His parents were torn, and while the letter seemed genuine, the McRobertses were filled with conflict: Was the writer telling the truth? Are these heartfelt words? Was Greg's death an accident, his body and bike concealed on the side of the road for weeks? Or were the rumors true? There is only one person who can answer that question. Only the letter writer knows what happened that night.

Greg's parents weren't alone in their conflicted feelings. Once again, people were talking, they were speculating, and they were calling law enforcement with their thoughts about what happened. Midland County sheriff's detectives ran down each lead.

Amy and Greg's two children read the letter, and like Greg's parents, they wanted to know more about that night, particularly regarding the rumors of Greg being taken from the scene after the accident.

The McRoberts family continues to hope that the writer will contact them once more to give them the peace they seek. Greg's surviving siblings tried to comfort and console their parents, but it was not to be. In the years after the letter's arrival, Greg's father was diagnosed with cancer, passing away in April 2016.

Greg's family is not alone in struggling to come to terms with his death. That is clear from the 2005 letter.

If you are from the Midland area or lived there at the time of the accident, you may know the letter writer, the man (or woman) who yearns to live a better life for themself and Greg's memory.

The writer is likely a Midland native or, at a minimum, lived there in the early 1990s. It is thought that at the time of the accident, the writer was driving a late model Oldsmobile, model years 1982–86.

From the letter, we know that the writer has a brother, has spent time in Minnesota, worked on a twelve-step program, and may still be in recovery and/or have a sponsor. The writer could also be a sponsor to a person or persons working the program.

The writer is divorced and could be particularly religious, a devoted Christian.

Greg's partner, the mother of his two children, passed away in September 2017. Amy and Greg are finally together again.

Greg's case is being handled by the Midland County Sheriff's Office: 989-839-4600

6

DEBRA RENTSCHLER

1980

In the summer of 1980, Detroit hosted the Republican National Convention. Former President Gerald Ford and future President Ronald Reagan stayed at the recently completed hotel inside the Renaissance Center, a futuristic glass tower of a building. It was an exciting time in the city, but for eighteen-year-old Debra Rentschler, Detroit was a place to work—a corner to stand on.

Debra's life hadn't been easy. Her mother died when she was young, and her father couldn't help his children process their grief. Debra was shuttled from one relative's house to another, and then as she got older, she stayed with friends.

Trouble found Debra, or maybe she found trouble.

As a teen in the 1970s, Debra was in and out of juvenile detention. By the winter of 1980, she was legally an adult, pretty and dark-haired, living in a dingy motel off Woodward Ave near Seven Mile Road and engaging in sex work to make ends meet. According to a 1981 story in the *Farmington Observer*, Debra had a criminal record. She'd been arrested for solicitation in November 1979.

One could say Debra had a boyfriend, but he wasn't her boyfriend, he was her pimp. He looked out for Debra, providing protection, making sure she was fed and there was a roof over her head, even if it was in a flophouse of a motel.

Christmas was coming. Debra had called her brother earlier in the week and said she would see him at Christmas.[2] He was happy to know that he would soon see his sister. Until Christmas, though, there was work to do, guys to party with, and money to be made.

It was after two in the morning on December 24 when Debra left the Euclid Hotel. The now-demolished structure was located just a block off Woodward Avenue. Debra's boyfriend was escorting her outside when he got distracted, maybe by one of the men who also lived in the hotel asking about a ball game or another of his girls needing attention.

Whatever distracted him, when he refocused his attention toward Debra, she was gone, vanished into the bitterly cold December night. He didn't think much of it. Maybe she'd left with a customer who beckoned her into the warmth of his car.

When morning broke and Debra wasn't back, the boyfriend was worried. He was concerned about her safety; in 1980, the working girls of Detroit were being preyed on—sex work is a dangerous occupation.

After hours passed without any sign of Debra, he reported her disappearance to Detroit police. Officers took the report but figured that she would turn up. The officer taking the report on the petite brunette likely felt a pang of concern; he'd seen what could happen to working girls who'd gotten in a car with the wrong guy.

Twenty miles and an entire universe away from Woodward Avenue in Detroit is the city of Farmington. As the name suggests, it started as a farming community in the 1800s.

Farmington is situated along Grand River Avenue, the main road between Detroit and the state capital of Lansing. In 1980, Farmington was a bedroom community, a suburb known for its charming downtown and Victorian-era homes dotting quiet, tree-lined streets.

About a block south of the main road that slices Farmington neatly in two is a low-rise brown brick building. This was the home of a light industrial business and an ironworkers' union hall. The building is set back from the road, off a tree-lined entrance.

Christmas Eve was likely the last day of work that week for the men and women employed in this building. At eight o'clock in the morning that Wednesday, a man headed into the building saw what he thought was a mannequin crumpled in the snow near the dumpster.

As he drew closer, he realized that it wasn't a mannequin. It was the body of a dark-haired white woman. As Debra's boyfriend had hours earlier, he went to the phone and called the police.

Farmington Public Safety responded quickly; the crime scene was less than a mile from the department. First, they cordoned off the scene and

The approximate location where Debra Rentschler's body was found. *Author's collection.*

then called in the Michigan State Police, who responded with a mobile crime scene unit. Investigators were careful, thoughtful, and thorough. Soon a team from the medical examiner's office arrived and carried Debra's remains out of the cold and into the van.

Within hours, police knew her name, and they knew that she was last seen in Detroit the previous evening. Investigators knew someone had dumped her body, naked and exposed in an odd spot behind a building in the middle of the night.

According to a story in the *Farmington Observer*, Farmington Public Safety Director G. Robert Seifert believed that she was killed elsewhere and her body dumped in the Farmington parking lot.

Investigators checked weather reports, learning that snow started to fall around two o'clock, meaning Debra's body, which was dusted with snow, was left there at or after two o'clock to be covered the way it was.

It was Friday, December 26, when the medical examiner took a look at the remains of Debra Rentschler. Dr. Robert J. Sillery, who had worked for Oakland County for many years, was in charge that day.[3]

Sillery saw her tattoos, the words *luv me* crudely imprinted on her arm, the crosses on her wrists, and the heart near her shoulder.[4] He saw the bruises and the needle marks. He reviewed the report of how Debra was found, naked and exposed behind a building on Christmas Eve morning. He learned that her home address was in Detroit, in one of the neighborhoods off Woodward Avenue near Seven Mile Road.

The doctor learned all these things about Debra, and he marked the case, this very obvious murder, a case of chronic hepatitis and moved on to the next body awaiting his attention.

Back in Farmington, investigators were frustrated. The manner of death was not listed as homicide. An eighteen-year-old girl was found twenty miles from home, naked and dumped in a parking lot, and the medical examiner wouldn't label it a homicide.

Once again, the men and women of the Farmington Public Safety Department went to work making calls and talking to other medical examiners, trying to get her cause of death changed to homicide.

As if Debra's life hadn't been difficult enough, in February 1981, her body was exhumed and transported to the University of Michigan Hospital in Ann Arbor.

There, not one but two medical examiners examined her remains. These physicians saw needle marks and her tattoos, but they spotted something obvious that Dr. Sillery had missed.

While Debra did have hepatitis and a history of drug use, there was more. Someone had taken her life by using a ligature around her neck; she had been strangled.

What investigators knew to be true all along was now on record. Debra's death was a murder.

While police searched for a suspect, no one saw who Debra left with the night she went missing. There was no vehicle description and no person to be on the lookout for.

In 1981, investigators didn't know the value of DNA. Slides, samples, swabs, and specimens were not collected meticulously as we see with today's more advanced technology.

As to tracing her belongings, Debra wasn't wearing jewelry that someone might pawn, nor was she carrying credit cards to be used. The few belongings found with her body were disposed of by law enforcement in the decades since her death.

The building where her body was found is still there today, but there are few houses nearby, meaning there were no witnesses to come forward with information. No one spotted a vehicle in the parking lot that night, nor did anyone see or hear anything suspicious.

As of this writing, Farmington Public Safety, led by Director Bob Houhanisin, is still working on the murder of Debra Rentschler. They are interested in any leads or information that might locate her killer and finally bring justice to her case.

If you have information on the murder of Debra Ann Rentschler, please contact Farmington Public Safety at 248-474-4700

7
EDDIE HOLLMAN
1992

In May 1992, Michigan native Eddie Hollman was twenty-one years old. Eddie dreamed of being a pilot, and after completing flight training in Oklahoma, he moved back in with his parents. On May 2, Eddie went out with friends. He arrived home around four o'clock in the morning and immediately headed downstairs to sleep on the sofa in the partially finished basement. He had only a few hours left to live.

Edward Arthur Hollman, known as Eddie, was the youngest of four children. He lived with his parents in a modest brick ranch in Wayne County, in the Detroit suburb of Dearborn Heights. The Hollman home was in the River Oaks subdivision, a welcoming neighborhood with a pool and community center. The Hollman house was in the northeast part of town, a stone's throw from the University of Michigan–Dearborn campus and Fairlane Town Center.

On May 3, 1992, Eddie's father, Ted Hollman, woke up shortly before six o'clock. His wife, Gina, got up a short time later. They made coffee and got ready for the promise of a warm spring day. The pair departed just after seven to attend the eight o'clock mass at Sacred Heart, a glorious cathedral located in Dearborn at the corner of Michigan and Military.

After attending morning mass, the Hollmans returned home for breakfast. The family had a day of work planned. It was spring cleaning weekend in their subdivision. Gina was president of the homeowner's association, and while Saturday was spent cleaning, mowing, planting, and organizing, there was always more work to be done. Ted visited the hardware store to pick up a few things. Gina decided to check the basement for supplies. But before we discuss Gina heading downstairs, let's talk about Eddie.

In 1992, Eddie was the only child still living at home. His older brothers and sister had all moved out; two of them were married with families of their own.

Eddie was an athletic, adventurous kid. He taught himself to play guitar; he learned to windsurf. In high school, he was on both the football and wrestling teams, where he earned a varsity letter. Outside of Dearborn High, he also played ice hockey. Eddie was a big guy, broad-shouldered and nearly six feet tall. He was a nice guy. Eddie was a jock, but he was friendly and likable, and he got along well with everyone.

Dearborn Heights is a strange place, geographically speaking. The north end of town is wide. Then the city narrows to a strip that's two miles long before it widens again toward the southern end of town. On a map, the city looks a little bit like a barbell running north to south. The city's irregular shape allows it to border the cities of Detroit, Dearborn, Garden City, Inkster, Redford, and Taylor. Dearborn Heights is half the geographic size and half the population of its sister city Dearborn.

While in high school, Eddie started dating a girl named Mara. Mara had a difficult home life, and at one point, Eddie asked his parents if she could move in with them. Concerned about Mara's well-being, the Hollmans welcomed her into their home.

The Hollmans were concerned about the reasons she left home. Gina recalled that Mara fell ill with the flu soon after she arrived.

While Mara was not the girl Gina Hollman wanted for her son, she knew Eddie and Mara were young, and these things had a way of working themselves out. Gina and her husband, Ted, watched as their relationship developed and changed.

After graduating high school, Eddie enrolled at nearby Henry Ford Community College, where he took classes while working a part-time job.

While Eddie enjoyed college, he wanted more than what a community college could offer. So, he enrolled in the Spartan School of Aeronautics in Tulsa, Oklahoma.

Mara moved with him to Oklahoma, and the couple shared an apartment while Eddie studied aviation and worked to obtain a pilot's license.

In 1990, the couple became engaged. Eddie didn't have the money to buy a fancy diamond ring like Mara was hoping for, so he purchased a cubic zirconia in a gold setting at the local Crowley's department store. Eddie popped the question to Mara on Christmas Day. The young couple toasted their future with a glass of champagne.

In 1991, Eddie earned his commercial pilot's license. Later that year, Eddie and Mara returned to Michigan. Gina traveled to Oklahoma to help the pair pack up and move out of their apartment. At the time, she noticed that things felt off between the couple.

Around the same time Eddie completed his pilot training, he broke off his relationship with Mara. Maybe it was the strain of being so far from home. Perhaps he realized that they wanted different things. Eddie and Mara agreed to stay friends, and they moved back to Michigan. Eddie returned to live with his parents, and Mara moved in with friends.

In January 1992, Eddie received twin-engine certification. Wanting to improve his flight skills, Eddie enrolled at Oakland Community College. His goal was to work as a flight instructor with his eye on eventually becoming a commercial pilot. Although Eddie had his pilot's license and completed his training, the law at the time stated that you had to be twenty-three years old to fly a commercial aircraft. Working as a flight instructor allowed him to fly frequently and hone his skills while helping others learn.

Several times a week, Eddie made the drive from Dearborn Heights north to the Oakland Community College campus for aviation classes and training at the Pontiac Airport.

The winter and spring of 1992 was a good time for Eddie. He was twenty-one and single. He had a part-time job at a men's clothing store and was making friends at his new school and the Oakland County airport.

The weekend of May 1, 1992, was all about old friends. On Friday, May 1, Eddie made the drive north to Mount Pleasant, home of Central Michigan University. Some of his high school buddies were students there, and they invited him to visit.

With Eddie in Oklahoma for much of 1991, he hadn't spent much time with friends from high school. Friday night was an evening of catching up with friends and partying. It was the end of the semester in Mount Pleasant, and Eddie's friends would be back at home in Dearborn Heights within a week or two. The guys had already started packing up their dorm room in anticipation of returning home for the summer. Eddie agreed to load some boxes into his car and transport them to Dearborn Heights.

When they woke up late on Saturday, Eddie told his friends that he needed to head home. They asked him to stay another night—there was more fun to be had. But Eddie passed. He wanted to get back to Dearborn Heights that afternoon. Eddie's friends had no idea that they would never see him alive again.

Saturday afternoon found Eddie back in Dearborn Heights. He saw his parents only briefly; they were working on community association business for the River Oaks Subdivision for their spring cleanup day. There was raking, mowing, and other yard work to be done, and the community pool needed to be ready for its opening over the upcoming Memorial Day weekend.

On Saturday afternoon, Eddie visited a friend's house to watch their band practice. These were people Eddie knew from high school, some of whom would be at the Saturday night party.

When Ted and Gina Hollman return home at five thirty that afternoon, they saw signs that Eddie had returned to the house, but it appeared he had already headed out for the evening.

Eddie went to a party in Dearborn with a friend named Pat whom he knew from high school.

Remember, Eddie was a nice guy and got along with almost everyone, moving between social cliques with ease. The people hosting the party was not his "jock" friends; they were from another clique, but again, many of them had known Eddie for years, some since elementary school. While at the party, Eddie drank heavily. Later, during his autopsy, his blood alcohol level was found to be well above the legal limit. There were no drugs found in Eddie's system.

Since he'd had a lot to drink, Eddie should not have driven home that night. But it's believed he made it back safely in the wee hours of Sunday morning. His dad, Ted, later said that he thought he heard Eddie arrive home around four o'clock. A few minutes later, his father heard someone, possibly Eddie, climb the basement stairs and use the bathroom on the first floor before returning to the basement.

Eddie often slept downstairs after a long night out. So this behavior did not raise any red flags for his parents. Like many Detroit-area homes, part of the Hollman basement was fixed up into a den, with a TV, sofa, and carpeting creating a casual living space. Just beyond the den area was a typical basement arrangement with a laundry room, workshop, and storage.

As was their routine on Sunday morning, Eddie's parents, Ted and Gina, attended early morning mass. After services, they returned home at about nine thirty. At just after ten, Gina went downstairs to gather some spray paint and stencils for the signs she needed to make for the community cleanup.

When Gina Hollman first lay eyes on Eddie, he was lying on his stomach on the carpeted floor near the sofa. His face was turned toward the television. There was a fluff of black fabric around his shoulders. Something about her youngest child didn't look right. As she crept closer, she realized Eddie's face was discolored. He was clearly not breathing.

Gina cried out and raced up the stairs. She rushed outside to a neighbor's house for help and frantically called 911. Police and an ambulance were quickly dispatched.

Meanwhile, Ted Hollman was at the hardware store, picking up a few things and looking forward to a productive Sunday with his family. He had no idea what was waiting for him at home. Eddie was Ted's only biological child.

When paramedics arrived at the Hollman home, they checked Eddie for signs of life. Rather than disturb what appeared to be a suspicious death, they placed a stethoscope on his back and checked for signs of respiration or a heartbeat.

But twenty-one-year-old Edward Arthur Hollman—son, brother, friend—was gone.

Officers on the scene notified the Dearborn Heights detective bureau of a suspicious death. When the detectives arrived, they took a close look at the body. There was blood near Eddie's left elbow and blood pooling beneath his nose. Eddie's body was face down on the floor with his arms bent at the elbows, his hands beneath his torso, and his face turned toward the television.

Gina never forgot her son's face. It was discolored and puffy. There were marks on his face consistent with Eddie trying to free himself from the makeshift noose that was wound around his neck. This included a laceration on his forehead and a contusion on one of his cheeks.

Dearborn Heights police notified the coroner's office. Detectives tried to determine if there were signs of a struggle or if this was a case of suicide. Nothing in the basement pointed to one cause of death or the other.

Detectives rolled Eddie's body over onto his back and discovered that the leg of a pair of exercise pants was knotted tightly around his neck. Working off the possibility that Eddie took his own life, police explored the surrounding area, looking for a place where Eddie could have secured the pants to hang himself. They didn't find any furniture or even a ceiling beam capable of holding Eddie's weight, which meant it was unlikely that he did this to himself.

Wayne County Coroner Dr. Yung A. Chung arrived to examine the scene. Summoning a coroner directly to a crime scene is an unusual move in a suspicious death investigation.

Dr. Chung determined that this was a homicide. The scene was processed, pictures were taken, and evidence was collected. Police also impounded Eddie's Mustang, taking it to their department so it could be processed for evidence. Eddie's body remained in place for several hours as evidence technicians and crime scene analysts looked for clues.

When Ted and Gina Hollman were interviewed, they told the police that someone phoned the house around four o'clock that morning. But they weren't sure if Eddie answered the phone or if the caller disconnected. Phone records clarify what happened (more about that later).

Police not only took Eddie's car, but they also removed the carpet from the basement. They intended to process both for evidence.

Gina and Ted couldn't agree on exactly what time Eddie returned home that morning. Gina thought he came in closer to one, but Ted believed he heard him come in around four. They both agreed that someone called their home at four and that the phone rang only once.

Eddie's father, Ted, was a creature of habit. He woke up each day around five, and he didn't notice anything out of the ordinary as he went about his morning routine.

Because Eddie had a busy social weekend leading up to his death, detectives had a lot of people to track down and interview. This included his friends from Mount Pleasant, the ones he partied with on Friday night. They also needed anyone else who was at the party in Dearborn on Saturday night. There were dozens of twenty-somethings to locate, interview, and in some cases, polygraph. They arranged interviews with his family and neighbors in the River Oaks subdivision.

They talked to many of Eddie's closest friends, including his ex-fiancée, Mara. While it was known that the couple had been broken up for a few months, something else detectives learned was that Eddie was on the phone with her just a few hours before his body was found.

It's worth mentioning that since ending the engagement, Eddie was never lonely. He dated frequently, including rekindling a relationship with a young woman he dated back in high school before he met Mara.

Do you remember that four o'clock phone call? The Hollmans' phone records revealed that Eddie spoke to Mara on the phone in the early morning hours of May 3. According to Gina Hollman, Mara told her that Eddie sounded like himself during the call. He wasn't upset about anything, nor did he seem depressed.

Even in the days before social media, news of Eddie's murder spread like wildfire. Many of his friends from high school were back in town now that school was out for summer vacation. The phone lines were crackling with news of Eddie's death. This soon led to a lot of speculation about what happened.

In 1992, the police didn't have a digital trail to follow. People relied on telephone and word of mouth, which can be difficult to trace. The main group of witnesses were young, and they weren't particularly helpful.

It's been reported—and keep in mind, this is purely speculation—that guests at the Saturday night party were smoking marijuana. While pot isn't as big of a deal now, back then, a drug bust could land you in prison. This could have been a reason that people were hesitant to talk or claimed not to remember certain things from the night of Saturday, May 2, 1992.

While dozens of people were interviewed, there was no single suspect that stood out. No one for the police to focus on. Despite an active investigation, Eddie's case didn't move forward.

During the mid-1990s, Eddie's case went before a one-man grand jury. This means that instead of presenting the case to a panel of citizens, the case is presented to a judge. Unfortunately, many of those called to testify pleaded the Fifth Amendment, refusing to answer questions about their activities that night because it might incriminate them. Once again, the case did not move forward. Although the Dearborn Heights police did not forget about Eddie Hollman, without new leads, his case grew cold.

Despite a lack of progress by the police and the courts, Ted and Gina Hollman remained determined to seek justice for their son. They hired an attorney to represent their interests.

Over time, the Hollmans grew frustrated with the lack of progress in the investigation. So, they hired a private investigator to dig into the case. They contacted a man named Richard Walter, one of the cofounders of the Vidocq Society, a group of hundreds of retired police detectives, FBI agents, and other law enforcement who specialize in solving cold cases. Walter is best known for his work on the psychological profile of family annihilator John List. In the 1990s, Walter was a well-respected investigator. He developed a theory about the crime, which he shared with the family and Dearborn Heights police. However, the information he provided was still not enough to move Eddie's case forward.

There are multiple theories about the death of Edward Hollman: Could the killer or killers have followed Eddie home that night? Was it someone he knew? Maybe a friend with whom he had a disagreement that escalated into murder?

This theory seems unlikely, because the Hollman home was not big enough to prevent his parents from hearing an angry argument or struggle in the basement. It is suspected that the killer or killers knew the Hollmans' routine of attending early mass and let themselves into the house when Eddie was home alone.

Another theory is that Eddie was asleep on the sofa in the basement, a common practice for him on the weekend. Someone entered the house and came downstairs, striking him in the face, leaving a gouge on his forehead and a bruise on his cheek.

When Eddie rose to confront his attacker, he was struck again, this time on the back of the head, knocking him onto the floor. Or perhaps he was struck on the back of the head first, and then when he turned to confront his attacker, he was hit in the face.

The killer acted quickly, grabbing a pair of exercise pants from the nearby laundry area and knotting them tightly around Eddie's neck. It's believed that Eddie struggled but was unable to fight off his attacker.

The killer then took the time to arrange things downstairs. The basement was staged to make it look like Hollman took his own life. But the injuries to Eddie's head and face make this scenario unlikely.

The question is, who would want to do this to Eddie? What was the motive? Dearborn Heights detectives interviewed numerous witnesses. But no one could come up with a reason anyone would want to murder Eddie Hollman.

In a 1993 interview with the *Detroit News*, one of the detectives on the case said he believed the killer was someone local to the area, someone who knew Eddie Hollman, and that the murder was not drug related.

One of the things to consider about Eddie's death is that his parents weren't home for much of that morning. This indicates that the killer or killers likely knew their schedule. The killer also must have had access to the house. Ted Hollman was always careful to lock the house behind him when he left. Could this mean the person who murdered Eddie Hollman had a key to the house?

Or did the killer arrive earlier? If Eddie forgot to lock the door behind him when he returned home, the murderer could have slipped in through the side door and down to the basement where Eddie, still drunk from partying the night before, slept on the sofa, unaware that he had only minutes left to live.

One rumor circulating around the case is that there was a strange car seen on Eddie's street the morning of the murder. Could somebody from the party Eddie attended have followed him home? There is also talk of a suspicious phone call made regarding Eddie's death on the morning his body was found.

This brings us to today. In the thirty-plus years since Eddie Hollman was murdered, his friends have grown up and moved on; some of them have moved far away, leaving Michigan behind. Others remain in the area, just a few miles from where they grew up in Dearborn and Dearborn Heights. Hopefully, one day, some of the people who pled the fifth rather than testify about the death of their friend will be ready to speak up and finally reveal what they know about May 3, 1992.

The Dearborn Heights Police Department is handling the case of Eddie Hollman. If you have information, please contact Dearborn Heights police at 313-277-6770.

PART II
THE MISSING

8

BERNICE GRAY

1991

When you reach the end of October, you can sense the holidays coming. First Halloween, then Thanksgiving, and immediately after that is the messy shopping frenzy that paves the way to Christmas. Then the year glides to an end with the long-awaited New Year's Eve party or event to say farewell to the old and welcome a new year, with all its possibilities. Of course, I'm simplifying things. The holidays can be hectic and stressful. We've all been there, making our way through a tense or awkward holiday meal or family gathering. Christmas is often equated with a family dinner and a glittering holiday tree, laden with gifts from Santa—but with those gifts come expectations and, sometimes, disappointments.

This case starts with someone not getting what they wanted for Christmas. But before arriving at the holidays, we need to talk about Bernice Gray and how a stressful Christmas led to her disappearance.

Twenty-three-year-old Bernice Gray was the only daughter of Jean and Tom Gray. She had a brother, Earl. In 1989, she became the mother of a daughter, Lindsay*. Lindsay was fathered by Bernice's much older boyfriend, Robert Pann.

Standing five feet, ten inches, and 140 pounds, Bernice had long brown hair and green eyes. She was a striking young woman, tall and smiling, her hair long and curly. She and her boyfriend, Robert Pann, had been together for almost four years. When she became pregnant with their daughter, the two moved in together. They shared Pann's canal-front home on Alexander Street in St. Clair Shores. With their first child on the way,

Robert suggested that they get married and make things official. Bernice wasn't ready for marriage. She didn't want to get married to him and felt she was too young. She had concerns, one of them being that she was nineteen to his thirty years old.

After Lindsay was born, the pair had their ups and downs. One of Bernice's friends said that she'd never seen Pann strike Bernice, but she described his temper, the anger that she'd witnessed from Robert, as "explosive."

As Christmas 1991 approached, Bernice realized that she couldn't stay with Robert. His temper, his mood swings—it was all too much for her. She worried about herself, and she worried about her tiny daughter. She thought she could make a go of things and have a family with him, but it wasn't working out. Bernice packed her belongings and took Lindsay home to live with her mother. Jean Gray was happy to have her daughter and grandchild stay with her.[5]

Christmas 1991 was unseasonably warm and sunny with few clouds and temperatures near forty degrees.[6] Not the white Christmas one may have wished for. Bernice woke on Christmas morning not with a sense of joy or childlike wonder but with anxiety and stress. On Christmas Eve, she'd

Bernice Gray took her toddler daughter and moved back home with her parents weeks before she vanished. *St. Clair Shores Police.*

turned down a marriage proposal from Pann, her longtime boyfriend and the father of her young child. While their relationship was over, she still had to see him and spend time with him. They had plans to go to her father's house on Christmas morning with the baby.

Despite her mood, Bernice dressed and put on a smile. Her daughter, Lindsay, was excited about the holiday and what presents Santa may have brought. Bernice was less excited about seeing Pann again, but they had plans to celebrate the holiday together. Pann drove Bernice, Lindsay, and Bernice's brother, Earl, to her father's house for breakfast. Her parents, Jean and Tom, had divorced back in 1984.

During breakfast, Pann confided in Tom Gray's lady friend that he'd proposed to Bernice on Christmas Eve, but she'd turned him down. Tom's friend later told police that Pann didn't seem angry or upset, and he presented Bernice's refusal of the ring in a matter-of-fact tone. Bernice's brother, Earl, who described Pann as somewhat of a friend (he'd done work for Pann as well as gone hunting and fishing with him), said that his sister and Pann were not getting along on Christmas Day. They weren't arguing, but they didn't seem happy with each other either. It was tense between Pann and Bernice, but they put on a good show for their little girl.

After breakfast with Bernice's dad, they headed back to her mother's house for Christmas dinner. Pann stuck around as long as possible, perhaps trying to persuade Bernice to change her mind about accepting the ring and his proposal.

Earl told police that it was nearly two o'clock in the morning when he saw Pann leave the family home on December 26, 1991. When Pann left the house, Bernice had less than five hours left to live.

The home Bernice shared with Pann and her mother's home were both located in the city of St. Clair Shores. St. Clair Shores is a suburb of Detroit located thirteen miles north of downtown. The city is known for its lakefront location and its well-known "Nautical Mile."

The Nautical Mile is a lakefront stretch of Jefferson Avenue between nine- and ten-mile roads; this section of Jefferson houses the Jefferson Beach Marina and several nautical-themed shops, bars, and restaurants, thus the nickname Nautical Mile.

Another distinctive feature of St. Clair Shores is that the city is home to more than fourteen miles of canals leading out to Lake St. Clair.

The house Bernice shared with Pann was on one of those canal-front streets, and there was a boat docked behind their home. Remember the canal-front location of Pann's home, as this will come up again later.

In 1991, Christmas fell on a Wednesday, which meant that on Boxing Day, Thursday, December 26, Bernice was back to work despite being up until the small hours talking with Pann. Keep in mind, her brother, Earl, saw Pann leave the house just before two o'clock in the morning on December 26. Bernice was up for work at five thirty. She was dressed and ready to go, as was her little girl, Lindsay. Bernice dropped Lindsay off with her daycare provider before heading to work in Southfield.

Once Lindsay was settled at daycare, Bernice got back in her car—a blue four-door 1989 Pontiac 6000—headed for the freeway. She'd pick up Interstate 696 to make it to the office by her start time of seven. With the stress of Christmas behind her, Bernice had one thing on her mind: a lunch date with her girlfriend, where she would be able to talk through the situation she faced with Pann. Bernice wanted to end the relationship, and he wasn't accepting her decision. He'd proposed marriage, and she turned him down flat.

Still, he was trying to keep their relationship alive. He'd asked Bernice to spend New Year's Eve with him as a date. She didn't know how to turn him down, especially since she had no other plans, but she didn't want to see him anymore.

Bernice was done. Done with the relationship and done with him. They had a child together, but she was moving on.

Late on Christmas night, during a phone call with the same friend she had lunch plans with, Bernice said she was going to figure out a way to get out of her date with Pann. She had no intention of spending New Year's Eve with him.

Seven o'clock in the morning arrived, and Bernice wasn't at work. Her boss, Kathy, noted that Bernice was not there yet. But Bernice did have a young child, and it was the day after Christmas, so Kathy decided to give Bernice some time. When she wasn't in by eight, Kathy called Bernice's home number. Kathy still had the Alexander Street number, the home Bernice shared with Robert Pann, on file, but there was no answer at the house. Kathy left a message on the answering machine at approximately 8:35 a.m. Around 8:45 a.m., Pann returned Kathy's call to tell her that Bernice spent the night at her mother's. He said Bernice was up late and suggested she was just moving slowly this morning.

Kathy then called Bernice's mother's home, and the call was answered by Sandy Ullmer. Sandy was engaged to Jean, which is why he answered the phone when Kathy called looking for Bernice. Sandy was concerned, because he heard Bernice and Lindsay leave the house on time that morning. There was no reason for Bernice not to be at work.

Sandy contacted Jean to tell her that Bernice didn't arrive at work. Jean was worried and called Lindsay's daycare. They confirmed that Bernice had dropped Lindsay off at six thirty. Everything seemed fine with Bernice when she dropped off her little girl.

Jean notified the St. Clair Shores police that Bernice was missing. She went to the station to file the report.[7] Bernice didn't make it to work, she missed her lunch date, and she didn't return to the daycare to pick up Lindsay. Jean took the baby back to her house and waited, hoping that Bernice would call or appear at the house. Jean called Pann, asking if he had seen Bernice. He told her that he had not. When he learned Bernice was missing, he didn't ask after his young daughter.

It was 1991. There were no cell phones, no texts, and no emails. Social media didn't exist. Word spread the old-fashioned way, with phone calls, conversations, and knocking on doors. Police took a missing person's report, and a description of Bernice, along with her blue Pontiac, was sent out.

When police contacted Pann, he told them that he spent the morning of December 26 at Lakeside Mall, a large indoor shopping center in Macomb County. His reason for visiting the mall? He was headed to a jewelry store to return the ring he'd offered to Bernice on Christmas Eve.[8] Bernice hadn't canceled her New Year's Eve plans with Pann yet. This meant there should have been hope for an engagement—unless, of course, Pann knew he wouldn't be seeing Bernice again.

After Pann's errands at the mall were complete, he went to work. He was meeting up with an employee to work at a client's home where they were building a wall in the basement. At this point there was no sign of foul play in Bernice's disappearance, St. Clair Shores police weren't taking any chances. They visited the home of Pann's client and asked to view the construction area while confirming Pann's report of being there doing work that day.

In Bernice's absence, her mother, Jean, cared for her young daughter, the almost two-year-old Lindsay. The weekend passed with no news of Bernice. Her family waited and hoped for an answer. For good news. For something better to tell a little girl who desperately wanted her mother.

On Monday, December 30, Bernice's car, the blue Pontiac, was found on Eastlawn Street on Detroit's east side. It was about ten miles south of the home Bernice shared with Pann. There were several boxes in the back seat of the vehicle, and the keys were dangling from the ignition. Police hoped Bernice's car would give them clues as to the whereabouts of the missing mother.

The Pontiac was filled with evidence, but not what anyone hoped to find. The interior of the car was bloodstained, and there was a .25-caliber shell casing on the front seat. They checked the trunk but found nothing of note. There was no sign of the missing mother. The vehicle was towed to the police station for processing.

Between the blood evidence and the shell casing, police believed this was foul play, not a mother who decided to leave voluntarily.

While checking on Pann, the police learned that he owned rental properties in the neighborhood near where Bernice's car was discovered. At the request of St. Clair Shores investigators, Pann came in for questioning. He reiterated that he didn't know what happened to Bernice, that he was worried about her, and he was not involved in her disappearance.

Gray's bloodstained Pontiac was found abandoned in Detroit. *St. Clair Shores Police.*

While Jean was praying for good news about the disappearance of her daughter and keeping track of baby Lindsay, the community rallied around her. A reward of $14,000 was raised, and the family of Robert Pann contributed $3,000 to the cause.

On January 2, 1992, braving the frigid weather, divers from the Macomb County Sheriff's Department took to the canal behind Pann's house in St. Clair Shores. While divers sought signs of Bernice Gray, officers searched inside Pann's house for evidence that could link him to her disappearance and possible murder. There was no sign of her in the house, on Pann's boat, or in the canal.

Macomb County law enforcement reached out to renowned expert Werner Spitz asking that he take a look at Bernice's Pontiac 6000 and give his thoughts. When Spitz looked the vehicle over, it was his professional opinion that, per the blood evidence, Bernice was shot in the head while seated behind the wheel of the car.[9] Then someone, most likely the shooter, pushed her into the passenger seat and drove the car away.

Law enforcement collected blood samples from Tom and Jean Gray so they could verify that the blood in the vehicle belonged to their daughter, Bernice. The tests took weeks to complete, as this was the state of technology in 1992. In March, the lab confirmed that the blood in the car belonged to Bernice Gray. Her family's hope that she would return to them, safe and whole, had faded. It was a grim realization.

Meanwhile, police were reinterviewing anyone who had contact with Bernice between Christmas Eve and the morning of December 26. In talking with her family and friends, the police learned that Bernice had recently broken things off with Pann and that—despite her moving out and taking the baby with her—he'd proposed to her on Christmas Eve. Bernice turned him down because she didn't want to marry him. As far as she was concerned, their relationship was over. Bernice's friends thought she may have met someone new and possibly been on a date with a new guy in the week before her disappearance.

When the police asked Pann again about his alibi, he told the officers that he left home around nine o'clock that morning, headed to a jewelry store inside Lakeside Mall, and returned the ring he'd used to propose to Bernice. Then he went to work with one of his employees.

As 1992 progressed, there was no sign of Bernice. Lindsay, her toddler daughter, missed her mother fiercely, and Jean tried to comfort and soothe the girl. They were together in their love and longing for Bernice.

The community was aware of Bernice's case, and they were suspicious of Robert Pann. In mid-January, a call came in that there was what looked like a grave on one of Pann's properties in Warren. The area was searched, but no remains were found. In early February, one of Pann's neighbors called the police to report that Pann rushed across the street one morning to catch the garbage truck, leaving just one bag of trash in front of his neighbor's house for pickup, rather than setting it at the curb in front of his home.

In late February, a woman in New Baltimore, a community in northern Macomb County, called police to report finding a torn-up address book in the trash outside of her business. The address book was notable because it contained Bernice Gray's name and phone number.

In May 1992, Bernice should have been celebrating her birthday, but she was still missing. The community was still focused on her absence, and Pann's neighbors were keeping an eye on him. A call came in to St. Clair Shores police advising them that Pann and his mother were unloading a truckload of bricks into the house. The neighbor straight-up told the police, "He could be using the bricks to hide a body."

In the summer of 1992, Pann started a relationship with a married woman, Linda Jozwiak. The woman's husband, Mark, came across his wife drinking with Pann at a bar in Roseville. While Jozwiak was keeping an eye on his wife and Pann, he saw them kissing. Jozwiak confronted his wife, and the two left together. They went home to talk about their marriage and relationship. Ultimately, Jozwiak thought it was settled, that his wife wouldn't see Pann anymore.

A couple of weeks later, Jozwiak stopped at home midafternoon to find his wife's vehicle at the house, but the home was locked up and quiet. When he entered, he saw a pair of men's shoes on the floor in the living room. They didn't belong to him. He called out for his wife, but there was no response. He went upstairs to the bedroom and found her in bed. She was half-dressed and told him that she was sleeping, so she didn't hear him come in.

At this point, Jozwiak noticed that there was a man's watch on the nightstand. Again, it was not his watch. Convinced that Linda was deceiving him, he called out for Pann to show himself. There was no response. Jozwiak grew angry and stormed down the stairs and out the back door to the deck. Linda, upset with her husband, followed him outside, where the two argued with yelling and raised voices. There may have been some pushing as well.

Just then, the back door was flung open, and Pann appeared. He was wielding a crowbar and bellowed, "I'm gonna kill you!" Pann struck Jozwiak several times in the head, shoulders, and back before Jozwiak caught hold of the weapon. At this point, a neighbor intervened by taking away the crowbar and ending the fight.[10]

Jozwiak filed assault charges against Pann. Afterward, he headed to the hospital to be checked for a concussion and for a doctor to look at the torn skin on his ear.

St. Clair Shores police interviewed Mark Jozwiak. They asked him if it was Pann who assaulted him. He said that he was certain it was. When asked how he knew, Jozwiak said that Pann was on the news about his missing girlfriend. Jozwiak asked his wife if that was the guy she knew, and she told him to turn off the television. Jozwiak said to her, "The police said he's a suspect in the disappearance." Linda replied, "The police don't know what they're talking about."

Pann's assault on Jozwiak happened just weeks after police completed their searches of Pann's property in Warren looking for Bernice's remains. They searched property off Hoover Road and another property off Bunert Road. No sign of Gray was discovered. Another of Pann's properties, this one near 9 Mile and Groesbeck, was searched without success.

While Pann was carrying on an affair with a married woman, he was also trying to regain custody of his daughter, Lindsay. Since Bernice's disappearance, Lindsay had lived with her new primary caretaker and grandmother Jean. When Pann filed for custody, Jean got creative. She called on the Chippewa Indian Tribe for support of her adoption of Lindsay.[11]

Macomb County Circuit Court Judge Frederick Balkwill heard the custody case between Pann, who was on bond because of the assault charges pending in Detroit, and Jean.[12]

Balkwill agreed with Jean, because she is a part of the Chippewa tribe, and therefore so were Bernice and Lindsay. He determined a tribal court should decide who would maintain custody of the girl. At the hearing, a tribal registrar testified that Bernice's great-great-grandfather was 100 percent Chippewa Indian. Therefore, Bernice and her daughter were considered members of the tribe. After the hearing, one of the tribal judges stated publicly that the tribe looked favorably on grandparent adoptions.[13]

Eventually, Jean was awarded full custody of Lindsay.[14]

Sadly, by the year's end, Bernice's case, which provided no shortage of evidence and several promising leads, wasn't going anywhere. It was not forgotten, but unless they found her body or additional evidence of Pann's involvement, there wouldn't be an arrest.

In 1993, Pann was in legal trouble again. He hadn't assaulted anyone, but he was charged with defrauding an insurance company. Pann faced charges of fraud, false pretenses, and perjury. As when Pann assaulted Mark Jozwiak, it is believed that he didn't serve any jail time. This case is not related to the disappearance of Bernice Gray.

Just ten days after the insurance fraud charges were filed, a specialized recovery group arrived in Michigan to search for Bernice's remains. A Colorado-based company called NecroSearch reexamined areas previously searched by law enforcement to see if anything was missed or if any sign of the missing woman could be located.[15] The search was unsuccessful. As 1994 began, Bernice was still missing.

There was no further mention of Bernice's case in the press until the fall of 1994, when her sweet, smiling face was again in the newspaper.[16] She was featured alongside other missing women from Michigan: Paige Renkoski (see chapter 12) and Jan Pattinson. As an aside, both women are still missing as of this writing, thirty-plus years later.

In this news story, Jean Gray, now Jean Ullmer, was pictured alongside her husband, Sandy, and her former husband, Bernice's father, Tom Gray. The three were working together to find Bernice and raise their beloved granddaughter. In January 1995, Bernice Gray was declared legally dead.[17] The ruling was made by a judge in Macomb County Probate Court. While Bernice being declared dead meant that her daughter, Lindsay, was eligible for benefits, it was an emotional time for her family. Jean told the press that they were thinking of buying a grave for Bernice. While they don't have her remains, a stone would mark her place in the world. Perhaps a memorial service could be held to celebrate her life and memory.

In the fall of 1995, Pann, who could not seem to stay out of trouble, made the news again.[18] His house, the canal-front home on Alexander Street that he once shared with Bernice, was cited because his boat was sinking in the canal. It was a nuisance and a hazard because engine oil and fuel were leaking into the water. The catch was that the boat didn't technically belong to Pann. Back in 1990, Pann was in a car accident in Woodhaven, Michigan. The day after the accident, Pann transferred the boat's title from his name to Bernice Gray, hoping to protect the asset if there was a lawsuit from the accident. With Bernice dead, she could not be the owner of the boat. After authorities attempted to reach Pann several times, a notice was posted at his house because officials were unable to locate him.

At one point in the sinking boat saga, police approached Pann's mother about the boat. The coast guard told her the boat was leaking oil and fuel and there needed to be a cleanup. Police were recording their interaction with her, and Mrs. Pann stated, "That boat was his pride and joy, then he kills her, and don't transfer the fucking thing into his own name!" Not only was the utterance witnessed by a St. Clair Shores police officer and a member of the Detroit Marine Safety Office, but it was also caught on tape and entered into evidence.

Sadly, there wasn't enough to arrest Pann for the murder of Bernice Gray. Not yet, anyway.

St. Clair Shores police were keeping an eye on Pann, waiting for him to do or say something that would give them a break in Bernice's disappearance.

Sometime between 1992 and 1996, Pann married Maureen Pann. She was to be the next victim of his anger. It was April 1995 when Robert hid in the back of her car and then popped out while she was driving and began beating her. This time, Pann wasn't given a bond or probation.[19] Pann was held in jail for months awaiting his trial. His wife, Maureen, just wanted this to go away. She didn't want her husband prosecuted for the attack.

Per her initial statements, the attack happened as follows: Maureen Pann got behind the wheel of her car and began driving. Her husband made his presence known in the back seat of the vehicle by grabbing her neck and yelling at her.[20] Then he started to punch her. She pulled the car to the side of the road while he struck her and repeatedly told her, "I'm going to kill you! You're going to die!"[21] When a police officer approached the vehicle, Pann sped away. He was eventually captured and taken into custody.

At a court hearing for the charges, Pann and his attorney sought a change of venue, claiming that Pann couldn't get a fair shake in Macomb County. A judge denied his request.

When the trial began, Maureen was called to testify. She frequently responded to questions about the incident by saying, "I can't remember," or "I exaggerated." Her hopes of sparing Pann from serious jail time were dashed. In January 1997, Pann was sentenced to six years in prison for felonious driving and aggravated assault with great bodily harm. He would have to serve at least three or four years in prison.[22]

When the verdict was announced, the Detroit newspapers ran a story and interviewed St. Clair Shores Detective Tom Jenny about the case. He worked on Bernice's disappearance for years and wanted nothing more than to close this case.

With Pann in prison, police and the prosecutor had more time to assemble a case against him for the murder of Bernice Gray on December 26, 1991.

In 2000, after working closely with law enforcement and the Gray family, Macomb County Prosecutor Stephen Kaplan filed charges against Pann in the death of Bernice Gray. A trial was set for January 2001. It had been nearly a decade since Bernice vanished, but with the attack on Maureen Pann, which also happened while she was behind the wheel of a car, Pann demonstrated a pattern of attacking women in vehicles. The attack on Mark Jozwiak years earlier also demonstrated his propensity for violence and his temper. A report completed by Dr. Werner Spitz showed that the blood in Bernice's Pontiac belonged to her. The trajectory and amount of blood made it highly unlikely that Bernice survived the gunshot that led to the blood spray.

MOUNT CLEMENS IS THE county seat of Macomb County. It was settled in the first half of the nineteenth century and was best known for its mineral baths. The bathhouses drew tourists to the area, including notables such as Babe Ruth, Clark Gable, Mae West, and publishing magnate William Randolph Hearst. The baths were rumored to have healing properties, and up until the 1970s, people traveled to Mount Clemens to experience a restorative soak. It's in this historic city that Robert Pann was tried for the murder of Bernice Gray.

On Friday, January 5, 2001, Macomb County Prosecutor Stephen Kaplan told a jury that he would prove to them that Robert Pann was responsible for the murder and disappearance of Bernice Gray in December 1991. Pann's attorney, Dennis Johnston, countered that investigators focused only on Pann, an innocent man, and there was no physical evidence linking Pann to the case.[23]

Trying Pann for the murder of Bernice without recovering her remains was a big gamble. Macomb County hadn't seen a case like this before, and the press was watching closely. Investigators were also aware that in less than three months, in March 2001, Pann would be up for parole. If they couldn't make this case, he would likely be a free man. Gray's family believed in Prosecutor Stephen Kaplan. They trusted that he could present this case in a way that would let the jury see what became of their precious Bernice.

Kaplan assembled his case, starting with Pann's whereabouts on December 26, 1991, the day that Bernice Gray disappeared. Pann was angry with Bernice for leaving him, for rejecting his marriage proposal, and for taking away his daughter. Pann was alone at his home on Alexander Street in St. Clair Shores that morning. The first contact he had with anyone was a phone call he made to his employee around 7:30 a.m., asking if he could work that day. Then Pann missed a phone call from Bernice's supervisor at 8:34 a.m. He returned her supervisor's call at 8:47 a.m.

Receipts from the jewelry store at Lakeside Mall show Pann entering to return the ring at 9:37 a.m. and leaving the store about 9:45 a.m. When Bernice's family came to his home at 10:00 a.m. to get Lindsay's car seat, Pann was at the house with his employee. The two men headed to a job, which was finished at about 2:00 p.m. Then Pann dropped the employee at his home. No one saw or spoke to Pann between 3:00 p.m. and a phone call with his mother in Florida at 9:30 p.m. When asked to help distribute fliers for Bernice the night of December 26, he said he was tired from work because he was digging all day. That doesn't jibe with what he was doing at work, which was putting up a wall in a client's basement.

On December 30, Pann arrived at the St. Clair Shores police station on his own. During questioning by police, he described his day, waking at seven, calling his employee, going to the mall, installing a wall at a client's house, and then heading home for a nap. Since he'd been with Bernice until two o'clock in the morning on December 26 and drank quite a bit on Christmas Day, he was tired.

Bernice's bloodstained car was recovered in Detroit midafternoon on December 30. By four o'clock that day, Pann's attorney had called the department, telling them that if they had any questions for Pann, they were to go through his office. With this information—plus the recorded spontaneous outburst from Pann's mother, among other evidence—Prosecutor Kaplan felt that he had what he needed to prosecute Pann for the murder of Bernice Gray.

On January 25, the case went to the jury. They heard the circumstantial evidence of Kaplan's case, including how Pann had several opportunities to get rid of Bernice's body, both using his boat or at one of the many properties he owned in the Detroit area. Pann also had access to and knowledge of using large digging machines like bulldozers, tractors, and graders.

For the defense, attorney Johnston hammered the point that it was all circumstantial. There was no evidence that Pann did anything to Bernice. No body, no crime.

The jury deliberated for two and a half days before returning a guilty verdict. They were swayed by the fact that on the morning of December 26, when Jean Gray came to Pann's home to get the car seat so she could pick up Lindsay because Bernice was missing, Pann didn't react. He didn't offer help, nor did he seem concerned about Bernice or his young child. Pann waited for days to speak to the police about his contact with Bernice before her disappearance, and when her car was found just a few blocks from one of his rental properties in Detroit, he immediately retained a lawyer and ceased cooperating with police.

Pann was found guilty of first-degree murder, and in Michigan, a first-degree murder conviction comes with a mandatory sentence of life in prison. Due to that sentencing structure, we may never know what happened to Bernice on that December morning in 1991. Since Pann remains in prison, he may never be compelled to reveal where her body is hidden.

In addition to life in prison, Pann was ordered to pay the Gray family more than $100,000 in restitution. If he wins a lottery or inherits any money, it will go to Bernice's family. The Gray family will receive the proceeds if he sells one of his many properties, like the rental homes in Detroit or the canal-front house in St. Clair Shores.

At the time of this writing, Robert Pann is in his late sixties and resides at the Carson City correctional facility in west Michigan.

If you have information about what became of Bernice Gray, please contact the St. Clair Shores Police Department.

In a tragic addendum to the disappearance of Bernice Gray, her cousin Garnet Lennox was murdered in Detroit in 2007. The case of Lennox, a father of two and beloved brother and son, remains open and unsolved.[24]

9

JODY BRANT

1994

Jody Brant was still a child when she disappeared in 1994. Her brother, Joe, described Jody as spunky and a free spirit, saying that she was tough and playful. You often hear victims of crime described as someone who just loved life. Well, for Jody, a pretty, blond teenager, it was true—she wasn't letting grass grow beneath her feet. Jody was out there doing and experiencing and enjoying.

The notion that the attractive teenage girl had a zest for living isn't a surprise. What is surprising is how thoroughly Jody disappeared. She was there one minute, a fair-haired girl with high cheekbones and a gorgeous smile. Then she was gone. Her car, a burned-out shell that used to be a Ford Escort, was the only sign she'd made it to Michigan. Before we get too far into her story, we need to talk about Toledo, Ohio.

The city of Toledo sits just south of the Michigan border, perched on the western edge of Lake Erie. Toledo straddles the Maumee River, and because a river cuts across Toledo, the city is dotted with bridges. Toledo is also a crossroads for several major freeways, including Interstate 75, the Ohio Turnpike, US 23, and US 24.

It's important to consider this tangle of roads, as they are central to our story. If you've ever driven through Toledo, it seems that the many highways, freeways, and tollways are perpetually under construction. If you aren't paying close attention or if you're distracted even for a moment, it's easy to become lost as you navigate across the city.

Memorial Day weekend 1994 wasn't the first time Jody made the long drive from her home in Georgia to her former home near Pontiac. Jody had friends in Michigan and family too. While a twelve-hour drive can be daunting, a determined teenager with a good stereo in her car might see it as an adventure.

Jody had a good stereo in her Ford. Her big brother, Joe, installed a new sound system complete with speakers and amps just weeks before her ill-fated trip.

It was a warm spring night, May 28, 1994, when Jody slipped out of her mother's home and drove off on a great adventure, leaving Georgia and her entire world behind forever.

In May 1994, Jody Brant was sixteen years old. She was the only daughter of Donna Gully, formerly Donna Jones, and her stepfather Robin Gully. Jody's father, who gave her the last name Brant, was not in the picture.

Late in the evening of May 27 or perhaps early on the following day, Jody slipped out of the house and got behind the wheel of her car.

She was heading north, back to Michigan. She had big plans to visit her cousins who lived in Waterford and Pontiac. On her way to Michigan, which is a straightforward trip north on Interstate 75, Jody found herself in Toledo, Ohio, in that tangle of highways and freeways and bridges and construction zones. It was nearly six o'clock in the evening when Jody placed a call, telling her family she thought she was lost and she was not sure where to go.

During the phone call, she told them that she thought she was in Erie, which is a small city in southeast Michigan, just off US 24. Jody may have thought she was still in Ohio, but she was likely a few miles over the border into Michigan. If Jody was in Erie when she made that call, she wasn't going the wrong way, nor was she lost.

Jody was likely in an unfamiliar area and not on the freeway. She could have quite literally driven north on 24, which turns into Telegraph Road, and taken it to the Pontiac/Waterford border, putting her close to where she was meeting with her family. But we don't know what happened next because sometime between Jody's phone call to report that she'd become lost and ten o'clock the night of May 28, Jody disappeared along with her car.

Jody was missing, and the Ford Escort with the stereo system lovingly installed by her big brother was set on fire. The blackened shell of the car was discovered early on May 29 with no sign of the pretty, popular, free-spirited Jody Brant inside of or near the vehicle. When Jody didn't arrive at her family's home in Pontiac by the evening of the twenty-ninth, her family left Georgia to search for her.

All her family knows is that their girl is missing. In these days before computer systems were commonly used by law enforcement, no one had made a connection between the burned-out car and the missing girl. A missing person's report for Jody was filed with Pontiac police, and unfortunately, it took a couple of days to link the burned-out Ford to Jody's disappearance.

Adding a layer of complexity to her case, this wasn't Jody's first trip from Georgia to Michigan that week. Just three days before she vanished, Jody, along with two male friends, made the twelve-hour drive north. Now you could call this a work trip or a business arrangement, if you will. Jody's car, her much-loved Ford Escort, was loaded with ten pounds of marijuana, and Jody was paid a couple of hundred dollars to make the drive from Georgia to Oakland County, Michigan, to deliver the cargo.

This first trip transporting marijuana was a quick one—driving up, making the delivery, maybe sleeping for a couple of hours, and then driving back. According to the police file, this trip occurred just two days before Jody disappeared. When the police came calling on Jody's friends and family in Oakland County, it's possible there was both hesitation and confusion on their part.

Hesitation because they didn't want Jody to get in legal trouble for transporting drugs and confusion because well, they just saw her. They just spoke to her. It was a challenge for investigators to sort out which sightings took place during which of her two trips. When did Jody make a phone call? When did she leave a message on someone's answering machine?[25]

This situation also put Jody's family in Georgia in a difficult position. If they admitted to police that they knew Jody was transporting drugs, they could be in legal trouble as well, even if they'd tried to talk Jody out of it. Back in 1994, possession of marijuana, especially a large quantity, was a serious offense. It appears that investigators handling her disappearance set aside the drug issue and allowed people to speak freely in an attempt to find Jody and bring her home safely.

Jody's uncle Roy and her brother, Joe, had missing persons posters made up, and they raced north to Michigan to look for Jody. On the way, they stopped at rest areas to post fliers and ask if anyone had seen her. Once they arrived in Michigan, they spoke with family and Jody's friends, hoping she'd turn up. They worked with Pontiac police to come up with a list of people who knew Jody was in the area, and that's when Jody's car, her beloved Ford Escort, was recovered near Monroe.

According to the police file on her case, on Wednesday, June 1, the connection between the missing girl and the burned vehicle was made.

Michigan State Police sent a helicopter down from Lansing to scan the area around where her car was found. They were hoping for some sign of Jody, some clue about where she could be, but the search turned up nothing. They brought in a search team using specially trained dogs and scoured the area, hoping to find Jody. But the land search using dogs wasn't any more successful than the search with the helicopter.

When Joe looked at what was left of Jody's car, he noticed a dent in the rear bumper that wasn't there before her trip to Michigan.

Could Jody have been the victim of an abduction? Someone could have bumped the back of her car to get her to pull over and then forced Jody out of the car at gunpoint. Her mother, Donna, clung to the idea that Jody was alive and well, that someone had her and perhaps she could be released. Jody could be found safe and returned to those who loved her. She was desperate for answers. According to the police file, Donna Gully consulted a psychic who told her that she saw Jody in Michigan and Jody was alive.

Sadly, in the thirty-some years since Jody's car was found on the side of the road in Whiteford Township, a singed remnant of what was once a Ford, there has been no sign of Jody.

The Michigan State Police were responsible for one part of her case, the burned-out car. The other part of the case, her disappearance, was being handled by Pontiac police. I should mention that Jody's family attempted to file a missing person's report in Georgia with the department where Jody lived, but the police in Georgia declined to take the case, suggesting that a report be filed in Michigan, which is what they did.

Jody's mother was not in any condition to cooperate with law enforcement. According to the family, Donna struggled with addiction on and off for years, and Jody's disappearance caused her to relapse. Donna turned to her vices as a coping mechanism, and as they'd done in the past, Jody's uncle Roy and his wife stepped up to help.

According to police records, Jody's car was discovered, burned, and abandoned on Turk Road near Beck in Whiteford Township in Monroe County, Michigan. When the car was found, it was about seven o'clock in the morning on Sunday, May 29. The paint had burned off the license plate, so the officer couldn't see that it was not a Michigan plate.

When he ran the numbers through LEIN, the Law Enforcement Information Network, he realized that the car wasn't registered in Michigan, so he radioed in and asked that the plate be run down to see where it may have come from. It was then that they learned the car was attached to a missing teenager from Georgia and a helicopter search was requested of the area. They brought in a search team with dogs to try to track Jody, but searches were unsuccessful. The area where the car was left was isolated, surrounded by farmland. When police canvassed nearby homes, no one had seen or heard anything.

One of the homeowners remarked that their dog usually responded to strange cars or people in the area, but the dog was quiet all night long. The only trace left behind on Turk Road was a scorched patch of concrete where Jody's car sat as it burned. Jody's car was towed to an impound lot, where it was examined by Michigan State Police Fire Marshal Division.

Detective Sergeant Donald Warden determined that when the car was found, the key was in the ignition and the point of origin for the fire was the front seat and the passenger side floorboards.

Jody Brant stood just five foot three, and when she drove, she liked to pull the driver's seat close to the steering wheel. But according to the police file, when Warden examined the driver's seat, it was pushed back as though someone tall was the last to drive it.

Jody's family advised investigators that the mechanism to move the seat was broken. It would take some effort to move the seat back. If Jody were the last one driving the car, that's not the position the seat would've been left in. It appears that someone else, someone tall, drove the Ford to that isolated spot on Turk Road on the night of May 28.

In the car, police found the remains of Jody's suitcases, which were reduced to burned hinges and bits of fabric. Also in the vehicle was a melted cassette tape and a pile of burned car keys, likely what Jody was carrying on her key ring. Remember, the Ford's key was in the ignition. Both front seats of the car were consumed, and the back seat was badly charred. There was heat damage to the engine as well.

When Jody left for Michigan, she was wearing a white T-shirt, maybe with a cow print on the front, and light blue jeans, and she brought with her two pink suitcases, a pair of roller skates, and a pack of cigarettes.

According to the family, Jody also took along a telephone calling card. For those of you who don't remember the days before cell phones, if you wanted to make a call, you had to have change, maybe ten or twenty cents to make a local call, or if you were calling long distance, you could need several dollars.

Jody had a calling card, which is sort of like a debit card but for making phone calls; you dial your personal identification number before making your call. This allows you to make local and long-distance calls from any phone. Also, the calling card tracked calls, and investigators hoped that this calling card was the break they were looking for.

They wanted to see who Jody had called in the hours before her disappearance. The records were requested, but again, it was 1994. This was back before everything was available on a computer. Police had to wait for days. Meanwhile, a tip came in that a girl matching Jody's description was seen at a local fueling station. Remember, Jody's brother and uncle were driving from Georgia to Michigan, and they were putting up missing persons fliers along the way. When they stopped at a gas station along Interstate 75, they asked if they could post the flier, and the clerk recognized Jody's face.

The clerk told investigators that Jody came into the store on Saturday, May 28, during her shift, which ended at five in the afternoon. The clerk stated Jody used the pay phone in the parking lot. Police contacted Michigan Bell and asked for a record of calls made from that phone, but none of the calls logged were made to Jody's friends in Oakland County or to her family down in Georgia.

Michigan Bell advised police that if the call was made using a calling card, which we know Jody had, the call might not show up in their log. When the reports from the pay phone finally arrived, there was nothing unexpected, nothing of interest, and nothing pointing them to where Jody Brant could be.

There is an argument to be made for Jody leaving on her own. Jody had a history of using drugs at least recreationally, and her home life living with her mother, brother, and stepfather was unstable due to her mother's issues with addiction. Jody did have a solid support system with her uncle Roy and his wife, who did what they could to help her. There was also her brother, who was a loving and stable constant in her life.

After Jody made the call using her calling card, the call where she said she was lost and thought she was in Erie, she vanished, and her car was found badly burned with her belongings inside. It seems unlikely that Jody took off for a new life and left her car and all of her belongings behind.

According to police records, when Jody's brother saw the car sitting at the impound lot, he noticed a dent in the fender, a dent that wasn't there when Jody left for Michigan. It's possible that Jody, a pretty young woman traveling by herself, was intentionally hit by someone so she would pull over. Once she pulled over, the person who hit her could have overpowered Jody.

But before we continue, be aware that no one has ever been named a suspect or a person of interest in Jody's case. No one has ever been charged or arrested for anything surrounding Jody Brant's case.

In the weeks before she vanished, Jody Brant dropped out of high school. In the days before she vanished, she used her vehicle to transport drugs from Georgia to Michigan. She did this as a favor for her friend Roland.

She'd known Roland in Georgia, but he and his family left Georgia for Michigan, settling near Pontiac. According to the police file, sometime in early May 1994, maybe a week or two before Jody disappeared, Roland's father was murdered. Police apprehended the man responsible for the murder, and police interviewed Roland, his brothers, and the perpetrator, the man who murdered Roland's father, trying to connect this to Jody's disappearance, but nothing came of it.

Police were aware that Roland's family could have links to the drug trade, and it would make sense that his family would not want police to focus on them. Law enforcement encouraged the family to come forward with any information they might have about Jody Brant, but they said they had no information to give. Roland and Jody were friends, and Jody may have been sweet on Roland. It did not appear that he had any knowledge or involvement in her disappearance.

There is one more theory to consider. Perhaps someone driving along the same route spotted Jody and her distinctive car with Georgia plates. Perhaps they thought she was on another drug run but alone this time, and she was run off the road to be robbed of her cargo. This would explain the dent and the bumper of her car. The problem is that the car contained only a teenage girl with her luggage and roller skates.

It seems unlikely that Jody ran off on her own. She made a point of paying for her car insurance a few days before her last drive. This left her with only a small amount of pocket money, and two, she loved that car. If Jody was going to take off, it would've been driving her little Ford.

Jody was last seen alive in Georgia. It is possible that only Jody's car made it to Michigan and Jody met with foul play long before she crossed the state line. When human remains are discovered in northern Ohio or southern Michigan, they're checked to see if Jody is a match. This first happened in August 1994, when the body of a young woman was found in Toledo, Ohio. The remains were checked against Jody's dental records, and it was not her.

Jody's case has been passed around a bit. Originally handled by the Pontiac Police Department, it was handed off to the Oakland County Sheriff's Department when the Pontiac Police Department was shut down back in 2011.[26] At that time, law enforcement services for Pontiac were moved to the Oakland County Sheriff's Office.

The disappearance of Jody Brant is a cold case. Her car yielded few clues; one clue was the driver's seat being pushed back. Jody's phone card, the calling card investigators hoped would provide clues and give them direction, didn't offer anything of value. Jody's mother, who struggled for years with addiction, lost her battle in 1995, leaving only Jody's brother, Joe, and her uncle Roy to continue the search. They are, of course, assisted by Jody's many cousins and friends who remember the pretty, spirited, blond. The girl who packed a suitcase and her roller skates before making the drive north to Michigan.

In May 1994, Jody Brant was sixteen years old, five feet, three inches tall, and weighed about 117 pounds. Her hair was blond or light brown and fell past her shoulders. Her eyes were a sparkling green-blue, and Jody had two tattoos: *JB* tattooed on her thumb and a cross on her ankle. At the time of her disappearance, she was wearing a white T-shirt, blue jeans, and athletic shoes. She smoked Marlboro Light cigarettes.

If you have information about the disappearance of Jody Brant, please contact the Oakland County Sheriff's Office or the Michigan State Police Monroe Post.

10

CONNIE ROYCE

1990

This story takes us to Macomb County, Michigan, in the city of Mount Clemens, to a popular bar and nightspot called the Hayloft. Our subject, Connie Lynn Royce, formerly Connie Bostic, went missing from Mount Clemens on a Friday night in June 1990, walking away from friends with only the clothes on her back, never to be seen again.

Connie was living with her parents in Madison Heights at the time of her disappearance. After a short marriage, she returned to the family home to collect herself. In the months before her disappearance, Connie was dating someone and they'd even moved in together, but the relationship was not working out. The relationship ended with a loud verbal disagreement, and the police intervened. This fight was not physical, but there was a police record of the report from when they responded to the home where the argument happened. But by May 1990, that relationship was well and truly over.

Connie met someone new, a guy named Greg Wisneski*. They first met at a bar over Memorial Day weekend. They started a conversation and planned to go out for drinks on Friday, June 1.

That Friday, Connie got dressed up for her date. She fixed her dark blond hair, put on makeup, and slipped on a pretty, form-fitting black dress with a flared floral print skirt. Connie finished the outfit with a pair of black high-heeled shoes, grabbed her purse, and headed out.

Connie drove her car, a light-blue 1980 Chevy Citation, to Greg's apartment in the nearby city of Sterling Heights. She arrived at his place between eight thirty and nine o'clock. One of Greg's friends, Brad Sullivan*, was also at the apartment. The three of them had a couple of beers, priming the pump, so to speak, before heading out for the evening.

Connie left her Chevy at Greg's apartment, and they headed north to the Hayloft to continue their evening. In 1990, the Hayloft was a large and popular bar. It often had live music and was known for a great social scene.

One of the interesting things about the Hayloft is that it had video surveillance at the entrance. In 1990, surveillance equipment was expensive, and you did not often find it at bars. The cameras meant that everyone who entered the bar had their movements recorded by the surveillance system. In addition to being recorded, everyone who entered the Hayloft had to interact with the bouncer and pay a cover charge.

Connie, Greg, and Brad were seen at the bar, and while Connie's relationship with Greg was just beginning, you can tell from their body language that they like each other. She gently touched his back and his shoulder; the gesture appeared warm and affectionate.

When the trio entered the Hayloft, it was about ten o'clock. Once inside the bar, they got a table and ordered drinks from their server.

Exterior shot of the long-abandoned Hayloft Lounge in Mt. Clemens. The building has since been torn down. *Author's collection.*

The bouncer and the bartender later told police that nothing seemed amiss. There was no altercation, no drama. Just three people hanging out listening to music and having a couple of drinks.

It was about eleven when Greg excused himself from the table to use the restroom. This left Connie and Brad at the table. Connie abruptly announced, "I've got to get out of here," and walked away from Brad, leaving her shoes behind.[27]

Connie was barefoot; she left her black high-heeled shoes at the table. As Connie exited the bar, her gait flatfooted and awkward, her shoulder clipped the wall as she rounded the corner.

Just like that, Connie Lynn, the daughter of George and Mary Bostic, was gone.

Brad was surprised by Connie's announcement and her departure. He waited for Greg to return from the restroom and explained what happened. The pair left the bar to search for Connie, and when they didn't see her, they asked the bouncer, the parking lot attendant, and other patrons. Had anyone seen a blond in a black dress? But no one could tell them where Connie went.

The men returned to the bar and waited, hoping she would return. According to investigators, much of this activity is verified, not just by the videotape of the main entrance, but by staff at the bar who saw and interacted with the men that night.

Greg and Brad searched for Connie. They asked after her and they waited for her, but she didn't return. When they were interviewed by police a day later, their stories were consistent and lined up with what was reported by Hayloft staff. Connie left on her own, abandoning her handbag.

Greg and Brad searched outside the bar for her and then returned to the bar to wait, figuring she'd come back for her purse and shoes. When the bar finally closed at two, there was no sign of Connie. They took her belongings and headed back to Greg's place, where Connie's car, the blue Chevy, was parked right where she left it.

It took a day for her family to realize that Connie was missing. They went to the Madison Heights Police Department and filed a missing person's report. On June 6, 1990, her story made the newspaper, appearing on page 4 of the *Detroit Free Press*.

Police began checking with businesses in the area to see if anyone saw or spoke with Connie. Employees at a local pizzeria, located about a block from the Hayloft, thought they saw her.

Staff at the pizzeria reported that a woman matching her description was using the pay phone that night. Connie's distinctive dress with a black tank top and a floral print skirt helped her stand out from other women they might have seen.

Police tried to pull records from the pay phone, but they were unsuccessful. If Connie made a collect call from that phone, which seems likely, as she left the bar without her handbag, the call couldn't be tracked.

Employees at the pizzeria mentioned a brown, two-door Ford perhaps from the early 1970s that was parked near Connie when she was on the phone, but no one saw if she entered the car or if she left the area on foot.[28] Remember, it was Friday night at a pizzeria. That's a busy shift; they were focused on their work, not on traffic outside the building.

In 1990, computers were rare, but some people had them. Someone used their computer to create a missing person flier for Connie.

Connie's friends and family papered Mount Clemens with these fliers. The poster read in part, "last seen wearing a black mini dress walking from the Hayloft bar downtown Mount Clemens at 11:15 Friday night, June 1st, 1990."

The flier then asks that witnesses contact the Madison Heights Police Department. You see, because Connie lived in Madison Heights but was last seen in Mount Clemens, there was a period when both police departments worked on her case.

When Mount Clemens police spoke with a parking lot attendant and others outside of the Hayloft on Friday night, no one saw Connie leave the bar. The only sighting was at the pay phone near the pizzeria. This appeared to be a legitimate sighting. They heard from a witness that Connie was alone at a pay phone on Broadway near North River Road, walking toward the Holiday Inn.

How many petite blonds in a black dress with a floral skirt were roaming Mount Clemens that evening? Hopefully, there was only one. And where did she go from there?

While the police did try to get call records from the pay phone, they were unable to track the calls that Connie could have made. Collect calls may not have been tracked by Michigan Bell back in 1990. It's possible that Connie walked to the Holiday Inn thinking she'd wait in the lobby for whoever she called for a ride, a warm, well-lit place for her to hang out until her ride showed up.

While the pizzeria pay phone was one avenue to investigate, there were other things to consider. The Clinton River runs through Mount Clemens, winds, and twists its way east, eventually emptying into Anchor Bay or Lake St. Clair.

Could Connie have met her end in the water? This would make her disappearance a tragic accident.

The Clinton River is well-traveled, and in Michigan, June is prime boating season. The Clinton River skirts the south end of Selfridge Air Force Base, and Selfridge has been an active air base since its inception in 1917. In the days following her disappearance, divers went into the river to search for Connie's remains.

Divers also searched a nearby water treatment plant thinking she might have had an accident. But these searches did not turn up any sign of her after she went missing. A body in the river or those busy lakes would likely have been recovered.

Police from both Mount Clemens and Madison Heights interviewed everyone they could, including Connie's parents and siblings, Greg and Brad, employees from the Hayloft, her former boyfriend, and her former husband, but nothing led police to a suspect.

From all appearances, the people interviewed by the police were helpful and cooperative. Some people they interacted with were, shall we say, more interesting to law enforcement than others despite having an alibi for the time of her disappearance. But the result was the same. Connie was gone, and no one could find her.

Alternatively, what if someone offered Connie a ride? Picture her, a petite blond in a party dress walking alone through downtown Mount Clemens at eleven thirty on a Friday night. She had no jacket, no purse, and maybe she was not walking steadily.

If Connie accepted a ride, she could have gone anywhere, and it's not outside the realm of possibility that she was snatched, literally pulled into a vehicle and no one noticed.

Or if they did notice, perhaps they didn't realize what was happening to Connie. It is not impossible that an as-yet-unnamed predator was in Mount Clemens that evening.

In the days after Connie disappeared, her car remained at Greg's apartment, at least until her brother grabbed a spare set of keys and brought the car back to the Bostic home in Madison Heights.

Her parents waited by the phone. Connie's mother told the *Detroit News* that this was not like Connie. She wouldn't stay away without calling. Then June became July, and there was no more news about Connie, not in the paper and not from law enforcement.

Both departments worked on and followed up on leads. From 1990 to 1992, her parents offered up a reward fund with $3,000, hoping that someone would lead them to Connie.[29] But two years of working on the case, two years of a reward being offered, and Connie's case went cold. It didn't go cold for her friends or her family, but without any new information, there was nothing new to pursue, no avenues to run down.

In 2009, the Macomb County Sheriff's Department reopened her missing person case, and the case is now under the jurisdiction of the sheriff's department. To understand why the sheriff's department has the case, we have to go back to 2005.

Citing budget concerns, the Mount Clemens City Council voted to end police services for the city and contract with the sheriff's department. Initially, this was supposed to be a temporary move with a plan to review the change after five years.[30] In 2010, allowing the sheriff's department to patrol Mount Clemens was a good arrangement for the city and the county because even now, the Macomb County Sheriff's Office is still patrolling the city of Mount Clemens and has jurisdiction over the 1990 disappearance of Connie Lynn Royce.

Starting in 2009, the Macomb County Sheriff's Office again spoke with Connie's friends and family. Investigators went back to the people who saw her that night at the Hayloft. They reinterviewed her siblings, her parents, her date that night, Greg, and his friend Brad.

The men Connie was with on Friday, June 1, 1990, have not been in any legal trouble over the last thirty-five years, nor have they shown any indication that they could have been involved in Connie's disappearance. Video surveillance at the bar also backs up their lack of involvement. Both Greg and Brad looked for her outside after she left and then returned to Hayloft and waited for her return.

Also in 2009, the Macomb County Sheriff's Department performed searches of her family's property, including places owned by Connie's sister Georgia. In 2010, they searched a former family residence along the Clinton River off old Kerner Road in Clinton Township. Investigators even did some digging in the area, but no evidence of Connie was discovered.

Another frustrating aspect of her case is that Connie had so little with her when she vanished, just her clothing, no heavy or valuable jewelry, and no handbag with ID or credit cards. This left little for searchers to look for, few things left behind in the wake of her disappearance. There were no credit cards to be used at revealing locations, no valuable rings or a necklace to pawn.

Connie walked away with literally the clothes on her back, and this made her disappearance all the more mysterious.

So who was Connie Lynn Royce? Connie, whose maiden name was Bostic, was a 1984 graduate of Lamphere High School in Madison Heights, Michigan. She was the youngest daughter of four children. She had two older siblings, Georgia and Fred, who were more than a decade older than her. She also had a younger brother, Chuck, who was three years her junior.

Connie grew up in a modest ranch home on the northeast side of Madison Heights, and by age twenty-four, she'd been married and divorced. After the divorce, Connie moved back home with her parents, who, at the time of her disappearance, were older, in their sixties, and Connie's sister, Georgia, was already in her early forties. Following her divorce, Connie had a relationship with someone new, and this relationship lasted from the fall of 1989 through May 1990, perhaps for six or eight months.

At the tail end of this relationship, police were called to the home to intervene in a domestic dispute. There was no physical violence, but there was a lot of yelling, and the pair split up after this blowup.

But on May 30, just before she disappeared, the now former boyfriend reached out to her perhaps to reconnect, but Connie was not interested. It was clear she considered their relationship over. If you're wondering about the ex-boyfriend, because of course that's one of the first places you look, law enforcement did verify his alibi, and they checked the alibi of her former husband. Neither man appears to be a workable suspect in this case.

The incident that night at the Hayloft was not a one-off for Connie. She'd done something similar a few months earlier. For that, we go back to January or February 1990.

Connie quarreled with the previously mentioned boyfriend, and when they couldn't resolve it, she stomped off without her shoes. Of course, in this case, Connie did make it back home safely.

In the almost forty years since Connie vanished, numerous leads and tips have been followed up on. Dozens if not hundreds of witnesses have been interviewed. There have been news stories and missing posters, but not one bit of it has led to Connie.

The Hayloft, at 140 North Gratiot Avenue, where she was last seen, closed several years ago, and the pay phone outside what once was a pizzeria is long gone, but we are still looking for Connie.

Looking at social media, there is a page for graduates of Lamphere High School, Connie's alma mater, and Connie's story is shared there as well. Her friends and classmates wondered what became of the pretty, petite blond they had known from childhood. Alas, there are no answers in her case, but Connie is remembered and she is missed. Her case is being handled by the Macomb County Sheriff's Office.

11

CARLEE MORSE

2010

On a warm August night, fifteen-year-old Carlee Jade Morse left the apartment she shared with her mother and went for a late-night ride with two people she thought of as friends. The outcome of that ride was fatal, to quote the police report: "I've been unable to find one shred of information, one piece of evidence, one statement made, or one witness that could even remotely suggest that Carlee Morse is still alive.…I have not been contacted by anyone regarding the sighting, possible sighting, or rumored sighting of Carlee Morse, it is as if she has disappeared off the face of the earth."

Carlee's case began in Westland, a Detroit suburb in Wayne County. Westland is located, not surprisingly, west of the city of Detroit, and while early settlers came to the area inhabited by Potawatomi Indians in the 1820s, the city began to develop in the years after World War II, when subdivisions were created to provide homes for the employees at nearby factories in Wayne, Dearborn, and Detroit. Originally known as Nankin Township, after Westland Mall opened in 1965, joining Eastland and Northland Malls, township residents voted in May 1966 to form a city under the name Westland.

At the time of Carlee's disappearance, the city of Westland was middle class, with a population of approximately eighty-four thousand people. Westland is known for its shopping and a variety of public parks. It's a nice place to grow up.

In the summer of 2010, Carlee Morse was fifteen years old, standing about five feet tall and weighing less than one hundred pounds. Carlee was spirited and fun. She was also weeks away from returning to school. In September, she would have been a sophomore in high school.

Just after midnight on Friday, August 20, Carlee told her mom she couldn't sleep. She said she was going to step outside for some fresh air. This was the last time her mother, Lori, saw Carlee. When Lori woke up around two o'clock in the morning, Carlee had not returned.

On Friday evening, Lori Morse entered the Westland Police Department to file a report about her missing child. She spent much of Friday calling around to see where her daughter could be. No one had seen or heard from her. Lori was worried—Carlee hadn't run away before and her friends didn't know where she was.

Westland police took a report from Lori and entered Carlee's information into the Law Enforcement Information Network. They advised Lori to contact them if she heard from Carlee or had any information on where her daughter could be.

Carlee's distraught mother followed up with Westland police on an almost daily basis, hoping that they'd heard something about her missing child, but the month concluded and school began with no sign of her daughter.

When police accessed Carlee's phone records, they noted that all activity on Carlee's phone ended in the early morning hours of Friday, August 20. While this could mean something ominous, they had no evidence pointing them in one direction or another. Carlee Jade Morse was nowhere to be found, and no one had seen her.

In the days and weeks after her disappearance, Westland police worked with the media, getting stories out on her case in the *Westland Observer* newspaper and on the local Fox affiliate.

Police reached out to the neighboring cities of Canton and Garden City, where Carlee was known to have friends and sometimes hang out. They also contacted the Wayne County Sheriff's Office, and Carlee's missing person fliers were posted around the city, particularly in areas where her peers might see them.

Hines Drive is a two-lane road surrounded by woods, parks, and wetlands. It wanders leisurely in a mostly southwestern direction from Northville to Dearborn. It passes through Westland, not far from the apartment Carlee shared with her mother. Searches were conducted both on foot and on horseback. Hines Drive makes its way through Hines Park.

Hines Park is a perfect place to hide out, or if you've harmed someone, it's a good place to conceal a body. Westland's Officer Bobby was responsible for Carlee's case. On his days off, he visited Hines Park, combing the area for any sign of the missing girl.

With permission from Lori Morse, police thoroughly searched Carlee's bedroom and found Carlee's diaries. Reading through them, they learned of a teenager who was struggling and unhappy.

Police also found drug paraphernalia in Carlee's bedroom, including pipes, blunt wrappers, baggies, and a small clear bag with a black, tar-like substance inside. One of the officers thought this could have contained hash. The most startling discovery was a ledger, outlining various amounts of marijuana, how much she'd paid for it, how much she sold, and the money that she received or was owed to her. Based on what the police found in her bedroom, Carlee Morse, who turned fifteen three months before she disappeared, was involved in the drug trade.

Officers spoke with several of Carlee's friends and boys she knew or had dated. When officers tried to reach one of these boys, Justin Yoshikawa, they learned that he had recently moved out of state. Two months after Carlee walked out of her mother's apartment, Officer Bobby received a call from Justin.

Nineteen-year-old Justin was back in Michigan and heard police were looking for Carlee. Justin told the officer he had no contact with Carlee since she went missing. Justin revealed to the officer that Carlee was a "major drug dealer" and sometimes dealt with pounds of marijuana.

Justin decided to contact Westland police because he had an outstanding drug warrant. He was hoping that if he helped with the investigation into Carlee's case, the police would speak to the judge on his behalf.

During the conversation, Justin was helpful. He even promised to get the names of people Carlee might have been in contact with within the drug trade.

In late November, just before Thanksgiving, the Federal Bureau of Investigation contacted Westland police. Carlee's mother, understandably upset that her child was still missing, feared Westland's police weren't working on Carlee's case and they weren't taking her disappearance seriously, especially considering what was found in Carlee's bedroom. She was worried that because Carlee was involved in drugs, investigators wouldn't give her the same attention that a different missing teenager would receive.

Nothing could be further from the truth. Westland police worked on her case and followed up on tips and leads. Wanting to reassure the agent and Carlee's mother, investigators outlined the work they'd done.

Carlee's case had not been forgotten, and officers focused on new leads as they came in.

What investigators needed was time. They didn't realize this case would hinge on the testimony of a teenage girl, someone who hardly knew Carlee, who learned enough about her, and the circumstances of her disappearance, to seek the help of responsible adults. This girl, Penny*, and her mother, Denise*, broke the case wide open.

Denise was concerned about how her teenage daughter was handling life. Penny was facing unique stressors, and Denise wanted her daughter to be well-equipped to handle life's challenges. Denise arranged for Penny to work with a therapist who could help her daughter navigate her feelings and process the world around her in a healthy way.

Each week, Penny's mother took her to a therapy appointment. One day, Penny turned to her mother and asked, "If I tell my therapist something really serious, will she have to tell the police?" Denise was concerned and curious. What did her daughter know that could require intervention from law enforcement?

That's when the real story started to come out. One evening, Penny saw something on the news, a candlelight vigil for a missing girl, Carlee Morse of Westland. Penny's boyfriend, twenty-two-year-old Nick Cottrell, had spoken of Carlee. Nick talked about how he and his friend Justin and Carlee sold drugs together and Carlee kept the money, so Nick and Justin got rid of her.

Penny thought it was just a story, just a lot of talk, but then she learned that the missing girl was real. Penny was upset and looking to her mother for guidance. Penny told her mom that in September, not long after Carlee vanished, Nick and Justin took off for a few weeks, heading south. Nick and Justin didn't tell anyone they were leaving. The young men packed up and went to Alabama to stay with Justin's family.

When Nick returned to Michigan without Justin, he told Penny more and more about Carlee Morse.

Nick claimed that Justin killed Carlee because she was stealing money from their drug-dealing operation. Penny asked what the girl's name was, and he told her it was Carlee and that she lived in an apartment near the intersection of Warren and Venoy in Westland.

Penny told Nick that the story about the dead girl was upsetting and that she might talk with her therapist about it. Penny needed help processing what she'd heard; it was too much to handle. Nick begged her not to say anything to anyone about what he'd told her, that she could talk to him or keep it to herself.

Denise was concerned about what her daughter said, so she went to her local police department and told them the story. Everything her daughter told her. The officer listened to Denise. A tale of a missing girl, a drug deal, a murder.

A call was placed to the Westland Police Department advising them of Denise's story. Did it fit the case they were working on? Yes, Westland did have a case like that, a missing teenage girl, and the names Nick and Justin were familiar to investigators.

A meeting was arranged; Westland police needed to speak to Penny to get the story from her. Denise picked up her daughter and went to the Westland Police Department, where Penny and her mother sat down with Sergeant Serrano. Officer Bobby was away on jury duty, so while he'd worked on the case since August, he missed out on the interview.

Sergeants Adams and Serrano met with Penny and Denise to hear the whole story. As Penny spoke, police heard details of Carlee's disappearance that were never made public. Penny told the police and her mother that Nick didn't want to participate in the murder, but Justin insisted, saying that if Nick didn't help him, Justin might pay a late-night visit to Penny.

When investigators asked Penny when she first heard Nick speak of the murder, she said it was late August but before Nick's birthday, which was on September 2. Carlee Morse went missing in the early hours of August 20.

Penny told the police that Nick was a habitual liar, and at first, she didn't believe him. Penny thought this was another of his crazy stories. She didn't want to believe that her boyfriend could be involved in a murder, but now, knowing what she did, she thought Nick was telling her the truth.

Police asked Penny if Nick and Justin left Michigan in September because of the murder, and Penny said yes, she thought so. Penny said no one knew they were going except for Nick's mother, Tina Lowe.

Investigators asked Penny to tell them everything Nick said to her about the night Carlee was murdered. She said that she didn't know Justin very well; she met him for the first time at the beginning of August. She heard that Justin told Nick to clean out his car. Nick's Ford Escort had big speakers in the back seat; Justin told Nick to take them out. Then Nick and Justin filled the back seat of the car with boxes and dirty clothes, creating a place for Justin to hide. Then Justin gave Nick a CD for the car stereo and told him that when a certain song came on, he, Justin, would strangle Carlee while she was seated in the front passenger seat.

According to the police file, Justin told Nick to call Carlee and see if she "wanted to smoke a blunt." When Nick called her, Carlee did want to smoke, and he headed to her apartment. He'd been there before; he'd taken Justin to see Carlee on many occasions. When Nick pulled up outside of her building, Carlee came out and got in the car. She didn't know Justin was hiding under the clothing and junk piled in the back seat. Nick drove to a nearby park, and he and Carlee got out of the car, sat at one of the picnic tables, and smoked marijuana. Then they returned to the car, and that's when Justin popped out, wrapping a dog leash around Carlee's neck and strangling her.

Carlee fought back, struggling for breath. Justin yelled at Nick to hold her legs, and Nick did. Nick told Penny that Carlee looked at him as if to say "Why? Please help me" and she was screaming and struggling to break free. Penny told him she didn't want to hear anything else about it, and Nick stopped talking.

Penny told police that when Carlee stopped struggling, Nick drove off, driving aimlessly around with Carlee's body in the front passenger seat. Justin wanted to make sure that she was dead. Officers asked Penny if Nick said what Carlee was wearing, and she said Nick told her Carlee was barefoot, wearing a pair of shorts.

Then the course of the interview turned to Carlee's remains. How did Nick and Justin get rid of her body? According to what Nick told Penny, once Carlee was dead, they drove to a park, dug a hole, and buried her in it.

Another time Nick told her a different story, that they'd stuffed Carlee's body in a bag and dropped her in the landfill. The third version of the story was far more gruesome. He said that Justin and Nick took her body back to Nick's house because there were power tools. Justin went into the garage and dismembered Carlee's body, wrapping the pieces in black trash bags.

Meanwhile, as Penny was being interviewed and telling Westland police what she knew, her phone vibrated and beeped with messages from Nick. When interviewers inquired about the messages, Penny said Nick knew she was considering going to the police. Nick wanted to know when she went; he said he would go with her.

Penny didn't believe him. She thought Nick wanted to know if she went to the police so that he could get out of town.

Penny had a message she wanted the police to hear, and she opened her voicemail. She mentioned a message she'd saved from Nick's mother, Tina Lowe. According to the police file, one of the things Tina said to Penny was, "If you turn him in, you are turning yourself in, just remember that. Because you helped him…they're going to consider you an accessory, because you know too much. Just remember that."

Tina Lowe may have been trying to intimidate Penny to keep her from saying anything about the murder. Lowe was likely desperate to protect her son.

Sergeant Serrano told Penny that it sounded like Nick's mother knew about the murder. Penny nodded in agreement. She told law enforcement that she was there when Nick told his mother, "I did something really bad and someone's dead because of it." Penny witnessed this conversation, but she was not certain what else Nick revealed to Tina Lowe.

Then the police asked Penny the reason for the murder: Could it be because of drugs? Penny said she didn't think so; Justin and Carlee had a long history. The two had dated, and earlier in the year, maybe in May, they quarreled, which turned into a physical altercation where Carlee hit Justin in the face. She'd "pounded his face in." Justin's face was bruised and scratched after the fight. The bruises were prominent, and he had to wear sunglasses at his high school graduation. Months later, he was still angry about the assault.

Penny revealed that Carlee and Justin had an unhealthy relationship. She said that Carlee would call Justin and tell him she was going to kill herself. Justin rolled his eyes and said that whenever Carlee was "on something" she would talk about suicide. One time when this happened, Nick and Justin made Penny call Carlee to see if she was going to hurt herself. Carlee told Penny that she was just playing around and that she wasn't going to do anything.

When Nick and Justin left for down south back in September, the only person Nick told was his mother. Tina Lowe had recently bought a house for her son, and since he was leaving town, he wouldn't be able to move in. No one else, aside from his mother, knew that Nick and Justin were leaving.

The pair originally planned to go to Florida, but those plans fell through, so they went to Alabama to stay with Justin's mom and her family. While the two were in Alabama, Justin had some sort of "mental breakdown" and checked himself into a psychiatric hospital for two weeks. When Justin was in the hospital, Nick decided it was time to return to Michigan. He asked Penny to send him some money so he could make the drive back.

Police circled back to try to pin down when Penny knew that it was Carlee who was murdered. She told them that Nick spoke of the murder in August and again in late September, but it wasn't until December 3, 2010, when Justin's girlfriend, Misty*, called Penny to say that she came across a Facebook page for a missing girl. Penny looked at the page and put the name and the Venoy Pines apartments off Warren Road together and figured out this was the girl they'd killed. Penny told police that Misty and Justin were still dating and sometimes Justin stayed at Misty's house.

When police asked Penny if she knew that Carlee, Justin, and Nick were selling drugs, she said that she did. Nick told her that he asked his mother, Tina, for $500 so he could start his drug-dealing business and get on with his life. Tina allegedly gave him the money. The way Penny understood it, Nick gave Carlee that money, and she bought drugs from her dealers.

Remember, this is 2010, and medical marijuana wasn't a thing in Michigan at that time. Marijuana possession and consumption were illegal.

Carlee spent $500 on a quarter pound of marijuana. She and Nick divided the drugs, and each sold off what they had. Carlee sold her portion for about $1,000, and according to Nick, she didn't share the profits with him. Nick was angry and told Justin what happened. Justin told Nick not to worry, he would take care of it. Justin would get Nick's money.

Penny told the police she was in a relationship with Nick, but she was afraid of him. He had assaulted her previously; she even filed a police report but didn't follow through on prosecution.

Before concluding the interview, officers asked Penny if she knew what happened to Carlee's cell phone. Penny told them that Nick said he and Justin destroyed it after killing her.

The interview with Penny and her mother started around six thirty on Friday night and lasted for hours. When the interview ended, there was more work to be done. It was time to take Justin Yoshikawa and Nick Cottrell into custody.

When police arrived at the Canton home of Justin's girlfriend, they were hoping to find Justin. The detective from Westland was accompanied by an officer from the city of Canton as they knocked on the door. Misty answered, and they asked if Justin was there. Misty said that he was and let them into the house.

Police found Justin sitting on the couch. They asked him to stand so they could place him under arrest. Justin stood, but as the cuffs snapped closed over his wrists, his eyes rolled up and he sagged as if in a faint. The two officers caught him. Justin stirred, saying, "I'm fine! I'm OK!" and they began leading him to the door.

Misty called out, "What's going on? Why are they arresting you?" Justin sagged as if fainting again, and once again, if the officers weren't there to catch him, he would have hit the floor.

Police read Justin Yoshikawa his rights and loaded him into the back of a squad car, taking him to Westland PD for processing.

Once in custody, Yoshikawa agreed to talk and told them a story about how fifteen-year-old Carlee Morse had done him wrong. She'd been in a romantic relationship with him, but they argued about cheating and she hit him, giving him a black eye. Then, months later, the three of them—Morse, Nick Cottrell, and Justin Yoshikawa—decided to get their marijuana sales operation up and running. Justin claimed that Carlee cheated Nick out of money, leaving both Yoshikawa and Cottrell angry with her. That's when the two men decided they would kill her.

When asked where they disposed of Carlee's remains, Yoshikawa told police that they drove to Cottrell's house and put the car in the garage, so they could move her body into the trunk without it being seen. Then on Friday morning, they put her in a black trash bag and drove around for an hour or two. When they were in a remote area, they came across a church and pulled in, dropping her body, which was in a black plastic trash bag, into the dumpster. Yoshikawa couldn't remember where the church was, nor could he recall the name of the church.

Yoshikawa agreed to sign a written statement confirming what he'd told police about the incident.

Less than twenty-four hours after Penny and her mother sat down with law enforcement to share her long, strange story about the murder of Carlee Morse, Nick Cottrell was tracked to Taylor, a city neighboring Westland, where he was pulled over and taken into custody during a traffic stop.

This wasn't Cottrell's first rodeo; he had several previous convictions, including convictions for home invasion and the manufacture and distribution of methamphetamines and marijuana.

Police proceeded to Nick Cottrell's place, the home he went to with Justin Yoshikawa the night Carlee Morse disappeared. Even though almost four months had passed, investigators collected evidence from the garage, including pruning shears that had what looked like hair stuck in them, and long strands of hair from an orange bucket in the corner of the garage.

Inside the house, they took Nick's laptop; two of his cell phones; a third cell phone, which was broken; some receipts for gas and cell phone bills; and a partially completed State of Alabama Department of Human Resources food assistance application. Police impounded Nick's car, the 1998 Ford, so they could conduct a thorough search of the vehicle.

When Cottrell was interviewed, he told police that yes, he and Justin had talked about killing Carlee. Justin was angry with her for giving him a black eye just before his high school graduation, and Nick was afraid of Justin. Justin had threatened to harm Penny, Nick's girlfriend, if Nick said anything about what Justin did to Carlee. Justin told Nick he was watching Penny's house and would hurt her if Nick talked.

Nick told police that he was afraid Yoshikawa would kill him or kill his girlfriend if he didn't go along with the murder, and then after the murder, it was his fear of Justin that made him stay silent.

Police informed Nick that Justin was in custody and wouldn't be hurting anyone. This made him more willing to talk. Nick told them a story very close to what Penny told the police the day before. He said that Justin hid in the back of Nick's car and strangled Carlee Morse using a dog leash left behind by one of Justin's housemates. The story changed from Penny's version and Justin's version when it came to how they got rid of Carlee's body.

Cottrell said that they drove back to his house in Taylor and put the car in the garage; then Justin went to work on Carlee's body, breaking her joints and folding her small body into a black plastic garbage bag with a red drawstring.

The two men loaded her remains into the trunk of Nick's car and drove around looking for a place to dump her. They came across a church that was maybe near Monroe, Michigan (about thirty miles south of where they lived). Nick said he didn't know which church, that they were "driving blindly" and that he had to use GPS on his phone to get back home. Nick agreed to take a ride with the police to try to find the church where her body was left. Justin also took a ride with another officer another day. The two were unwilling or unable to lead police to the location where Carlee's remains were dumped.

One of the most frustrating things about this case is that neither Nick nor Justin offered a straight story about what became of Carlee's body. While it's possible that they were frightened and under the influence when they disposed of her remains, it seems unlikely that they'd forgotten where she was.

With Nick and Justin in custody, both having confessed to police their involvement in the murder, what officers wanted was to bring Carlee home, to find her remains so the Morse family could have that bit of closure and lay her to rest.

In addition to the ride-along with officers through areas that could be where Carlee was dumped, Justin and Nick were given supervised access to computers so they could look at aerial views of churches, hoping one of them would be where they'd left Carlee's remains, concealed in a black plastic trash bag. Without narrowing down the location where her body was, it was impossible to search the landfill for her remains. Westland police and the family of Carlee Morse still hoped to bring her home for a proper burial.

Even though there was no body and no blood evidence of a murder, the prosecutor was confident that they had a strong case against Yoshikawa and Cottrell. In addition to both men signing written confessions and talking with law enforcement about how the murder occurred, there was the testimony of Nick's girlfriend, Penny, and a new witness, Larry Jackson*.

Jackson told police that he'd recently become roommates with Nick. On December 8, he overheard an argument between Nick and Penny. The argument was over Nick's involvement in a murder and whether Penny would talk to someone about it.

Nick told Jackson he was afraid Penny would go to the police, booted up his computer, and showed Larry news stories online related to the Carlee Morse disappearance. Nick also told Jackson that Justin was using Penny as leverage; if Nick told anyone what happened, Penny would be harmed. Jackson asked Nick where the body was, and Nick responded, "Decomposing somewhere."

Police had voicemails and text messages from Nick's mother, Tina Lowe. They considered building a case against Lowe since she knew about the crime. While law enforcement were trying to decide how that should be handled, Nick's roommate Larry Jackson returned to the station with more information for detectives. In addition to his written statement about his interaction with Nick, he'd had a conversation with Tina Lowe.

According to the police file, Jackson said Lowe called him because she heard he'd spoken to the police. She wanted to know what he said to law enforcement. Jackson told her that the police had a warrant and searched the house. Lowe responded, "They couldn't have found anything because I cleaned the garage and took everything out."

Police asked Jackson if Lowe said what she meant by "everything," and Jackson said she didn't elaborate.

The officers involved in this case worked hard to locate Carlee Morse. They searched from Toledo, Ohio, to Northville, Michigan, and back again, checking dumpsters, cemeteries, Google Maps, and Hines Park. Her body could not be located. Neither Nick Cottrell nor Justin Yoshikawa gave a straight answer about where they left her remains. The story shifted and changed. None of the churches, schools, maps, or aerial photos looked familiar enough for either man to say *that's the place.*

A jailhouse informant housed with Cottrell said that Nick once asked him if you dump a body in Ohio and Ohio has the death penalty, could you get the death penalty too? The informant didn't have an answer for him.

What an interesting question Nick asked. Carlee's home in Westland was just fifty miles from the Michigan-Ohio border; it's possible they transported her body out of state for disposal.

Westland police met with the owner of a landfill in Flat Rock, Michigan. They wanted to look for Carlee's remains and wondered what that might involve. Police were informed that since a landfill can receive 250,000 tons of trash in a single day, it would be necessary to determine where the body was picked up if they were to have any hope of finding her remains.

The Center for Missing and Exploited Children was contacted, and they confirmed what the landfill owner told police; without a specific dumpster to start from, there is no reason to attempt a search of the landfill.

Police used GPS data from Cottrell and Yoshikawa's phones to attempt to narrow down their movements that night. The area they were left with was massive, stretching from Monroe, Michigan, south to Toledo, Ohio, and from US 23 east to Lake Erie.

Officers took photos of nearly one hundred churches in this area and showed them to Cottrell and Yoshikawa, hoping one would be the right location. When officers from other agencies learned of the Morse case, they offered suggestions and sent photos hoping to assist.

On February 3, 2011, Nick Cottrell struck a plea deal with the prosecutor's office and accepted a term of second-degree murder with a sentence of twenty-five to fifty years in prison.[31] Part of the plea agreement stated that Nick Cottrell must testify against Justin Yoshikawa during Yoshikawa's trial.

Cottrell's plea agreement also required him to tell the court about his role in the murder. Carlee's mother, Lori, and Carlee's sister, twenty-three-year-old Lauren, asked Cottrell to tell them where Carlee's body was. They begged him to give them an answer so their daughter and sister could be laid to rest, not left among trash in a landfill somewhere.

Cottrell's attorney, Solomon Radner, told the court that Cottrell had schizophrenia, bipolar disorder, and attention deficit disorder and was "scared to death" of Justin Yoshikawa.

During Cottrell's sentencing, the judge, Wayne County Circuit Court Judge Ulysses Boykin, said the phrase *heinous crime* is overused, but in this case, it fit.[32] That's when he handed down the twenty-five- to fifty-year

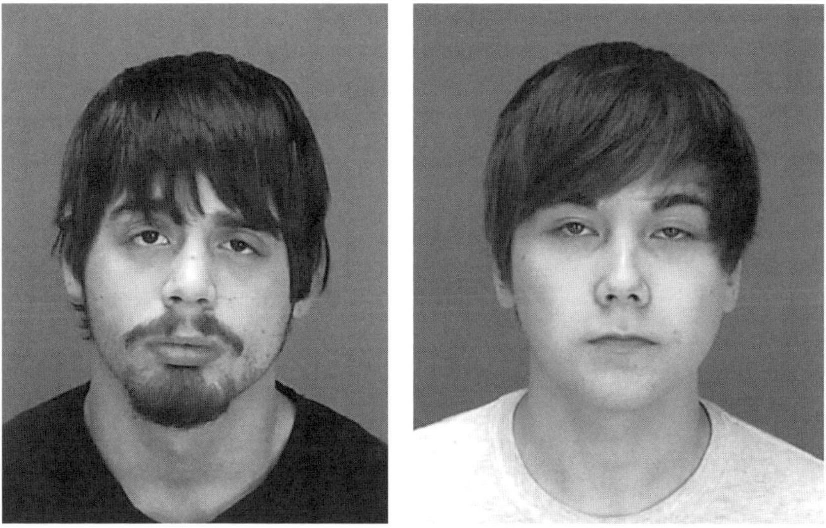

Nick Cottrell's (*left*) and Justin Yoshikawa's booking photos. *Westland Police Department.*

sentence for second-degree murder. One imagines that if Cottrell told the court where Carlee's remains could be found, the sentence might have been lighter. Cottrell's mother, Tina Lowe, was in court observing the sentencing of her son.

On Tuesday, August 8, 2011, Tina Lowe, the then-forty-nine-year-old mother of Nick Cottrell, faced charges of accessory after the fact to a felony and interfering with a police investigation.[33] Working with her attorney, the prosecutor offered Tina a plea. If she pleaded guilty to interfering with a police investigation, they would drop the accessory after the fact charge. Lowe and her attorney agreed, and Judge Boykin sentenced her to two years' probation and ordered her to pay $783 in court costs.

With a court date originally scheduled for July and then adjourned until October, plans to try Justin Yoshikawa for the murder of Carlee Jade Morse continued. Part of Nick Cottrell's plea deal stipulated that he testify against his friend in court.

On November 17, 2011, Nick announced that he didn't like his plea deal, and he wouldn't testify.

He'd spoken with another prisoner incarcerated for a similar crime and that prisoner received only eighteen years. Cottrell said that his deal "wasn't fair," and he wouldn't testify unless they reworked his plea and lessened the amount of time he must spend in prison. The prosecutor wasn't having it. He told Cottrell that wouldn't happen and advised the judge that Cottrell had backed out of his plea agreement.

The trial for Justin Yoshikawa began on Monday, November 21, 2011. With Cottrell refusing to testify, his earlier testimony from the plea hearing was read into the record. The jury listened intently. After consulting with his lawyer, Yoshikawa wanted to make a deal. Prosecutors spoke first with Carlee's mother and sister, to advise them that there could be a deal on the table. On Wednesday, November 23, 2011, Justin Yoshikawa accepted the plea of thirty-five to fifty years in prison for the murder of Carlee Morse. If he'd taken his chances with the jury, he could have faced life without parole.

This case is closed and neatly tied up. Two confessions, two men in jail. However, there has never been any information about the location of Carlee Jade Morse. She walked out of her apartment on a warm August night, never to be seen again.

Nick Cottrell and Justin Yoshikawa are legally responsible for her death and for concealing her remains. Unless one of them comes forward with information about the location of her body, she may never be recovered.

12

PAIGE RENKOSKI

1990

If you ask someone in Michigan what the best-known missing person case is, they will likely say that it's the 1975 disappearance of Jimmy Hoffa. Hoffa, the troubled former boss of the Teamsters Union, was supposed to have a two o'clock meeting on the afternoon of July 30, 1975, with the notorious alleged Mafia guy Anthony Giacalone, aka Tony Jack. At two thirty, Hoffa phoned his wife; he was annoyed that Tony Jack was late to the meeting and told her he'd be home by four to grill steaks for their dinner.

Hoffa was never seen again.

Hoffa's disappearance received an onslaught of media attention for decades after his disappearance. Today, some fifty years after he vanished, there are both wisecracks and questions about his case. We're going to look at another missing case, of a person less well-known but equally significant, the case of Paige Renkoski. Paige was last seen in May 1990.

Her disappearance happened fifteen years after Hoffa's fateful meeting at a restaurant on Telegraph Road. Paige wasn't famous; people didn't stop her on the street because they recognized her. However, her disappearance, the great mystery of her case, is compelling. This is an instance where one might entertain the notion that a UFO levitated her out of her vehicle and into thin air. Paige Renkoski disappeared completely.

She was last seen on a sunny afternoon in a busy place—the side of the interstate. In the middle of the day, she vanished from a well-traveled area. Paige left behind her shoes and her purse.

Paige's case has been looked at by law enforcement agencies from Michigan and beyond. There have been tips and leads. They've brought men and women in for questioning, and different investigative teams have looked at the file, then looked at it again. They're left with very little. How does this happen? How does a thirty-year-old vanish from the side of an interstate in the suburbs on a Thursday afternoon?

May 24, 1990, was a decidedly nice spring day in Michigan. The high reached seventy degrees, and warm temperatures paired with sunshine made for a lovely start to the long weekend. On Thursday afternoon, people were wrapping up their work week and excited about the long weekend that accompanies the holiday. Plenty of people were loading up cars for a weekend up north or pulling the tarp off the boat or the pool. It was here, Memorial Day weekend, the unofficial start of summer in Michigan.

Paige's mother, Ardis, was traveling. Two of her four daughters lived in Georgia; she had booked a flight to Atlanta and looked forward to spending quality time with her family. The Renkoski girls—Tami, Paige, Sheril, and Michele—were the pride and joy of Carl and Ardis.

With Tami and Michele living out of state, the long weekend brought a chance to visit and catch up. Ardis was looking forward to the trip.

The Renkoski family was based in Okemos, a suburb of Michigan's capital, Lansing. Ardis worked for an automotive supplier, and Carl, after serving in the military and working in law enforcement, took a job with the State of Michigan Department of Licensing and Registration. Ardis and Carl attended Michigan State University, and the family were fans of Spartan Athletics. The Renkoski girls enjoyed a typical suburban upbringing.

In the spring of 1990, the four Renkoski girls were adults. Grown and flown as they say. Thirty-year-old Paige was living with her fiancé, Steve Fillmore*, but still in close contact with her parents. Steve and Paige had been dating since 1987, when they met at a Michigan State Spartans hockey game.

When Paige graduated from high school in 1978, she wasn't sure what she wanted to do with her life. She did some modeling at local venues, attended college off and on, and worked as a substitute teacher. Nothing felt like the right fit for her. Eventually, Paige decided she wanted to be a teacher, to work with young children, and she returned to school while hoping to land a job in her field.

On May 24, 1990, Paige was up and about with a purpose. That morning, she dressed in a white blouse, colorful silk pants, and a beautiful beaded necklace. Her wavy, dark blond hair swung free around her face.

She had plans to drive her mother, Ardis, to Detroit Metropolitan Airport in Romulus, a few miles west of Detroit.

The trip from the Renkoski home in Okemos to the airport was about eighty-two miles, and since most of the trip was on the freeway, it should have taken just over ninety minutes. The route to the airport from Okemos was Interstate 96 to Interstate 275 to Interstate 94, which led almost directly to the terminal.

Ardis Renkoski later told police that on the ride to the airport, her daughter was fine and acting normal. She spoke of her fiancé having a softball game that afternoon. Paige told her mother that she was looking forward to the game, and it was likely that a group of them would head out afterward for dinner and a beer. When they said goodbye at the airport, neither mother nor daughter knew that this was the last time they would be together.

After dropping off her mother, Paige pulled away from the airport. She wasn't headed directly home, as she had plans to see a girlfriend who lived in Canton. Canton is located about ten miles north and west of the airport. Paige arrived at her friend's home, and they visited. Her friend had a child or young children, so they went to a local park so the adults could chat while the kids played.

The group also stopped for ice cream. It was a good visit, two friends catching up. When Paige said farewell—after all, she wanted to arrive in time for Steve's softball game that afternoon—nothing was out of the ordinary. Paige had not done or said anything that concerned her friend.

Paige stopped at a local party store before hitting the freeway, and she would take northbound I-275 to get home to Okemos.

At the party store, Paige purchased a cold forty-ounce beer. As she was making the purchase, the female clerk admired the colorful beaded necklace Paige was wearing, Paige smiled and thanked her. They chatted briefly, and then Paige was gone, getting into her car to continue her trip home. When news of Paige going missing reached the Detroit area via newspaper and TV broadcast, the party store clerk came forward to share her interaction with Paige. The information she provided to law enforcement proved helpful to investigators as they retraced Paige's movements.

On May 24, 1990, Paige wasn't driving her vehicle. The car that Paige was driving belonged to her mother, and that's not exactly right either. The car, a silver 1986 Oldsmobile Cutlass Calais, was her mother's work vehicle, so technically it belonged to the company she worked for.

After leaving the party store and getting into the Olds, Paige did something controversial. On that sunny Thursday afternoon, Paige took the cold forty-ounce beer she'd just purchased in the party store and poured some of it into a cup from a fast-food place. Then she put the remainder of the beer back in the bag, put the Cutlass in gear, and headed north on I-275. It was about two forty-five when Paige left the party store.

Paige was probably listening to the radio; she was likely feeling happy, headed to see her sweetheart play softball and then hang out with friends. There was a long holiday weekend ahead of them. She was excited about her engagement and had so many things to look forward to in the days, weeks, and months ahead.

While on the freeway, Paige stopped at a rest area to use the facilities. There is a reliable witness who saw her in the rest area, and after Paige disappeared, this woman contacted law enforcement with information. She said she saw Paige speaking to a man at the rest area. She offered a description of that man, which gave the police something to work with. The woman didn't describe the conversation as concerning; neither party looked upset, so she went on about her business and didn't give much thought to the two until she learned Paige was missing.

Paige did leave the rest area, continuing her trip home, but she never made it because something or someone stopped her.

Her vehicle, the silver Oldsmobile Cutlass Calais, pulled to the shoulder of the freeway. Paige exited the car and stood on the shoulder in her bare feet. Her hair moved in the breeze caused by cars as they whizzed past her.

She left behind her shoes and her purse. She left behind most of the beer she'd been drinking. Paige not only left the keys in the ignition of the vehicle but also left the car running. Why would Paige do that?

What would make Paige pull a functioning car to the side of the interstate? That's the first question. Why did Paige pull over? The car was working fine; it was working so well that hours later, when an officer pulled up behind it to tag it as an abandoned vehicle, he found it running. I can't say if he peeked inside the car to see a purse and shoes or if he opened the door and turned off the car. He did tag it and made a note of the interaction in his log.

You see, Paige Renkoski wasn't missing yet, no one had reported her. Steve was playing softball, laughing with his friends, and turning to look at the stands, checking out the onlookers hoping to catch a glimpse of his fiancée, but Paige didn't arrive.

After the game, there was no sign of Paige. She didn't join Steve and friends for a post-game dinner at a local place. There was no message on their answering machine either. It's 1990; there are no cell phones to check. Paige just wasn't there.

Eventually, Steve placed a call; he placed several calls. *Has anyone seen Paige?* The answer, time and again, was no. No one had seen her; no one had heard from her. That evening police were notified, and people began searching for her. Her friends, family, and loved ones papered the area with, quite literally, thousands of missing person posters hoping to find Paige.

As news of her disappearance made the papers and the TV news, calls started coming in. Witnesses reported that they saw her car, the silver Cutlass Calais, on the side of I-96 between three fifteen and four thirty that afternoon. The timeline fits. Paige left the party store in Canton around two forty-five.

The drive from the now-defunct party store to the area just before the Fowlerville exit where her car was found is about forty-six miles. This would take about forty minutes, depending on traffic and how fast Paige was driving, plus her stop at the rest area. It's not unrealistic to put her there at three thirty.

Why did Paige pull over? What made a thirty-year-old woman stop her car on the side of the freeway when the exit was nearby, a safer choice for her to pull off the road?

The Oldsmobile Paige was driving on May 24, 1990. Her purse and shoes were found inside the still-running vehicle. *Livingston County Sheriff's Department.*

We can discard the notion that Paige was having car trouble. The Cutlass was in fine working order when it was found. Remember, the vehicle was running when it was discovered by law enforcement that afternoon.

What if someone faked an accident? Could a person in another vehicle have tapped Paige's bumper to get her to pull over and then overpowered her? Investigators say her vehicle appeared undamaged. One of the investigators pointed out that the reason for these bump accidents, where people are forced to pull over, is to get money from the other driver. Paige's purse and wallet were untouched. If you're thinking about her bank accounts, Paige was not a wealthy woman, but she did have some money in savings; her accounts were never accessed. No one ever attempted to obtain any of that money.

Did Paige, zipping along with I-96 traffic at speeds of sixty or seventy miles an hour, see someone she knew, and then decided to pull off to the side of the road? But Paige's vehicle was one hundred yards or so from a convenient freeway exit. If you see someone you know, wouldn't you pull over to chat somewhere safer than the side of a busy freeway?

Another theory is that Paige walked away on her own. She planned her disappearance. However, if Paige was leaving her life, why drive back home? At Metro Airport, or even in Canton, she's less than an hour from the state line, so why not point the car south and keep going? Or, if she wanted to disappear while closer to home, surely she would at least take her shoes and purse with her.

Paige, like many women, carried a handbag, and the handbag was a lifeline. It is where she kept the money, her makeup, ID, credit cards, checkbook, lip balm, and breath mints. If you're leaving, these are items you take with you.

Paige did not need to escape. She was engaged to be married, her life was good, and she was happy. It wasn't perfect—few lives are—but there was nothing for Paige to get away from. Hours before she disappeared, Paige told both her mother and her friend that she was looking forward to Steve's softball game and the holiday weekend ahead.

This leads us to Steve Fillmore, Paige's fiancé—could he have been involved in what became of Paige? He was at his softball game with friends that afternoon, at the exact time that Paige went missing.

After the softball game, when Paige was a no-show, he went to her mother's house. Paige's parents had split up in the early 1980s.

At the home of Ardis Renkoski, Steve knocked on the door. When he didn't receive an answer, he let himself in, looking for his fiancée. According

An aerial view of the Fowlerville exit. Paige's car was found a few hundred yards from the off-ramp. *Livingston County Sheriff's Department.*

to a story on January 12, 1994, in the *Livingston County Daily Press and Argus*, what Steve found was an answering machine with a blinking light telling him there were unplayed messages.

Steve listened to the messages, hoping to hear from Paige. Instead, he heard a deputy from the Livingston County sheriff's office reporting that Ardis's car, the 1986 Oldsmobile, was found on the side of the freeway. Steve drove to the sheriff's department and told them Paige was driving that car and she was missing.

There is a common misconception that police won't do anything unless a person is missing for twenty-four hours, and that's not true. A search was started to locate Paige. Because Steve was her fiancé, he immediately became a person of interest in her case. Law enforcement cleared him, and her family never entertained the idea that he could have brought harm to Paige.

It's safe to cross Steve Fillmore off the suspect list. He wasn't just looked at and cleared once; he was checked out several times over the years. Steve still lives and works in Michigan and is in contact with Paige's family.

When we look at the tips and leads called in to investigators, one vehicle was described time and again, a minivan. The minivan was described as burgundy or dark red.

As we try to narrow down what kind of minivan it was, consider that the first iteration of commercially successful minivans originated with the Dodge Caravan and Plymouth Voyager in 1984. General Motors and Ford quickly followed with minivans of their own, such as the Chevrolet Astro, the GMC Safari, and the Ford Aerostar.

We can't forget that there were other minivan options from foreign brands like the Mazda MPV and the Toyota van, among others. In the Detroit area, the minivan seen near Paige and her vehicle was likely made by one of the big three, but we cannot eliminate the possibility that it was an import. When police looked up dark-red Mazda minivans trying to narrow down the suspect list, they learned there were more than one hundred of them registered in the state of Michigan. Trying to narrow the field via vehicle description was a time-consuming and frustrating process.

The last theory in the case is one built around eyewitness testimony. Before we explore this theory, we need to talk about Paige's father, Carl Renkoski. Paige was raised by a man who worked in law enforcement for more than a decade, including as a military policeman in the 1950s and later as a police officer for the Michigan State University Police Service. Paige and her sisters were raised to respect people in positions of authority.

What if someone pulled up alongside Paige on I-96 and showed her a badge before pointing for her to pull over? It's possible she followed the instructions of this unknown person or persons with a badge, never imagining that they were an impostor.

When Paige pulled to the side of the freeway, the other vehicle also pulled over.

Now, there are varying eyewitness accounts of this scenario. Did the vehicle, possibly a burgundy minivan, pull in behind Paige? Was the van occupied by more than one person? Was the driver of the van Black or Latino male?

One scenario has the vehicle stopping in front of Paige and the man with the badge walking toward her car, his arm outstretched, elbow bent, palm forward.

If you're trying to picture this, imagine that you are holding up your hand in a gesture for someone to stop, and then imagine that you are holding a badge in the palm of that hand. This is the description given by an off-duty member of law enforcement who passed what he believes was Paige and the person or persons responsible for her abduction.

This witness was traveling in the other direction and saw them for just a moment as he passed by. The stance of the man jumped out to him; it appeared he was showing Paige a badge.

Another eyewitness described a dark-skinned man, likely Black but possibly of Latino descent, speaking with Paige near her car on the side of the freeway and then taking her by the elbow, leading her away. Keep in mind that the people offering these sightings to law enforcement are reporting something they saw for a few seconds as they passed by at sixty or seventy miles an hour.

The use of a badge to get Paige to comply could mean that someone connected to or formerly connected to law enforcement was involved in the abduction of Paige Renkoski. It could also be someone who obtained a badge or a reasonable imitation of one and passed themselves off as an officer. This phenomenon isn't uncommon, and we'll get back to that in a moment.

The idea that someone used a badge and presented himself as a police officer could explain why Paige cooperated and pulled off to the shoulder of the freeway. Paige's sister Michele stated, "That is my top theory. Because there were rumors on the news or in the paper, I don't even remember exactly where. But during that time period, maybe a year or two, whether it was prior to her missing or after, that there were reports of someone, I don't know, a sixty-mile radius that has been badging, flashing a badge, and getting people to pull over. I don't recall exactly when or where that was, but that was a topic of conversation as a possibility, which would make more sense."

If someone was passing himself off as an officer, it's possible Paige pulled over thinking she was following the law. By the time she realized that the person who flashed the badge had misrepresented himself, she couldn't get out of the situation.

It's baffling why Paige left her shoes and purse behind in her vehicle. Why not turn off the car? Did he show her a weapon in addition to the badge? Perhaps a gun tucked into his waistband? Did he tell her something, words shouted over the buzz of traffic whizzing by that made her follow his instructions without hesitation?

If you're thinking that people masquerading as law enforcement doesn't happen that often, there was a high-profile case of this in the Detroit area in February 2020, when Oakland County Sheriff Michael Bouchard was on his way home from work and spotted a vehicle, a dark Ford Explorer, with a "Police Interceptor" label on the back, "call 911" on the rear quarter panel, and "emergency response" on the driver's door.[34]

Sheriff Bouchard activated the lights on his vehicle and pulled the driver over. As he walked up to the car, the driver put down his window and said, "Who are you?"

Bouchard responded, "I'm the sheriff, who are you?" A search of the vehicle turned up a semiautomatic handgun and a large, sheathed bowie knife as well as a fake police computer, a fake radar setup, and a set of flashing lights, illegal equipment for a personal vehicle.

UPON REVIEW OF PAIGE'S case, with the little that we know and all the questions we are left with, it certainly seems possible that Paige was approached by someone impersonating an officer and lured from her vehicle under false pretenses.

Looking back at Paige's case across the decades, we don't know much more now than we did in the days after she disappeared. Police interviewed men they referred to as suspects. Specifically, in 2002, investigators spoke to a man serving time in prison. This was not the first time he'd spoken with investigators. He had a lot to say, including a discussion of possible involvement of himself and some of his associates in her disappearance.

One of those associates was a minor, age seventeen in May 1990. This suspect mentioned two other men, men whom law enforcement showed an interest in but have since died: One a victim of gun violence, the other died while serving an unrelated prison sentence. All four of these men have criminal records and ties to illegal activities in Detroit and the metro area.

The location where Paige was abducted, the side of I-96 near Fowlerville, is between Detroit and Lansing. Is it possible that this man, or this man along with some of his associates, saw Paige, an attractive blond woman driving alone, and flashed a badge at her, perhaps pointing to a problem with her vehicle? Maybe they told her that she had a tire going down.

Paige pulled her car to the side of the road and hopped out to check the condition of the tire. While Paige was standing barefoot beside her car, he showed the badge and placed a hand on her arm. As one of the witnesses told investigators, he took Paige by the elbow and led her back to his vehicle, perhaps the burgundy or maroon minivan that was seen by witnesses. What happened next, we cannot say, but it was nothing good, nothing you'd want to reflect on for very long. Paige was taken, and then she was gone.

We also need to acknowledge that Livingston County, where Paige was last seen, is known for Klan activity going back to the earliest part of the twentieth century. In 1990, most of the Klan was long gone, but the racial tensions remained. The idea of a van full of Black or Latino men kidnapping a white woman and driving around with her on the back roads of Livingston County is a risk many would not take.

Then again, these were men willing to pass themselves off as law enforcement. These were men with long criminal records, men who served time in prison, and, in one case, men who died because of gun violence. Where would this group of men have taken Paige? Where could they have safely disposed of her remains?

Law enforcement followed up on tips and leads as they came in. Cadaver dogs were used to search areas, and digs were performed, but there was nothing, no evidence, no clues, no sign of Paige.

At the time of her disappearance, Paige Renkoski was thirty years old, five feet, seven inches tall, with shoulder-length dark blond hair and blue eyes.

Paige had a surgical scar on her right arm, and her left knee had been replaced years before she went missing. There are two surgical screws in her left knee. When asked about the condition of Paige's knees, her sister Michele revealed that when Paige was in high school, she was goofing around on her kid sister's skateboard and took a bad fall, severely injuring her knees. These distinctive injuries and corrections would make it easier for remains to be identified should she be recovered.

In the weeks following Paige's disappearance, her father, Carl, suffered a grand mal seizure and was hospitalized for several days. He did recover and spoke to the *Detroit Free Press* on the first anniversary of her disappearance; he was looking for answers. His health continued to deteriorate, and Carl Renkoski fell ill and passed away in 1994 at age sixty-one, never learning what became of his daughter.

Paige's mother, Ardis, worked on behalf of not only Paige but also other families and victims for the next twenty-five years. Ardis volunteered with Parents of Murdered Children, and she helped form the Missing in Michigan organization in 2010.

Ardis worked closely with the University of North Texas and the NAMUS program. In 2015, Ardis was given the honor of being named the first Michigan State Police Missing in Michigan Advocate of the Year, an award that has subsequently been named the Ardis Renkoski Advocate of the Year Award. The list of her good works goes on and on.

Age progression photo of what Paige might look like today, as a woman in her sixties. *Livingston County Sheriff's Department.*

In the summer of 2017, Ardis was involved in an accident in which she suffered serious injuries. In December 2017, Ardis passed away at the age of eighty-four.

Law enforcement work and giving back to the community are family traditions. Paige's niece Nikki has shown an interest in following in the footsteps of her grandparents. She has a criminal justice degree and works as an advocate for children and families.

The friends and family of Paige Renkoski are still hoping for answers to her disappearance. If you have information on the case, even if you've spoken with law enforcement previously, please make the call. Paige's case is being handled by the Livingston County Sheriff's Office. You can reach the tip line at 517-546-8477.

PART III
THE DIG

13

THE MACOMB COUNTY DIG

2018

In the late spring of 2018, law enforcement agencies from across Michigan participated in what became known as the Macomb County Dig. Warren police took the lead on this project, and they were supported by other agencies, including the FBI and the Macomb County Sheriff's Department.

The dig occurred on a vacant parcel of land in Macomb Township, near 23 Mile Road and North Avenue. This property was in the news a decade earlier, in 2008, when, directed by a convicted murderer and known pedophile, investigators unearthed the body of missing teenager Cindy Zarzycki.

In 1986, Cindy Zarzycki was a pretty and athletic thirteen-year-old residing in East Detroit. Cindy loved music and creating mixtapes for friends. She loved to dance, sing, and play sports. Her parents divorced in 1980, and she lived with her father and siblings. Cindy saw her mom, Alice, quite frequently, and the pair had a good relationship.

One Saturday in April, Cindy told her father that on Sunday morning she would be attending church with her friend Kathy and Kathy's family. In reality, Cindy had made plans to see a boy she liked—Scott Ream. Cindy had a big crush on him, and Arthur Nelson Ream, Scott's father, invited the hazel-eyed teenager to attend a surprise birthday party for his son.

On the morning of Sunday, April 20, 1986, Cindy dressed, styled her hair, put on her favorite white boots, picked up her denim handbag, and set out for the Dairy Queen on Nine Mile Road. This was the agreed-on meeting place. The Dairy Queen is located a couple of miles east of the pay phone Kim King (chapter 14) may have used to call her sister back in 1979.

Cindy told her younger brother Eddie Jr. that she was going out for a while. Eddie asked where she was going and reminded her that she was grounded. Cindy told him to stay home, but Eddie followed her up the street asking her not to go. Cindy would not be dissuaded and left despite her brother's cautions.

Cindy Zarzycki was sweet on Scott Ream and wanted to be his girlfriend. Arthur Nelson Ream took advantage of this situation, telling Cindy that he was having a surprise birthday party for Scott. Cindy didn't know this was a lie; Scott's birthday was January 18.[35]

It appears that Ream planned this weekend carefully: He'd sent Scott out of state to visit with friends of the family. This way there could be no contact between Scott and Cindy that weekend.

We don't know what Ream told Cindy while in the van that morning, but he drove her to his carpet warehouse, where she was assaulted and murdered. He then buried Cindy's body on a plot of land in Macomb Township. Decades later, this location would be the site of the Macomb County Dig. The property, once owned by friends of Ream, was a place he was familiar with.

When Cindy didn't return that Sunday from her "church outing with Kathy," her family began a relentless search for answers. Eventually, Cindy's friend Kathy came clean and revealed Cindy's plan to go to a surprise party for Scott Ream.

Why Arthur Nelson Ream wasn't immediately a suspect in her disappearance remains a mystery. Ream had a criminal record and was a known assaulter of teenage girls.

Cindy's family was devastated by her disappearance; they pursued every avenue to bring her home safely. According to a June 1990 story in the *Detroit Free Press*, they put classified ads in newspapers asking "Cindy Jo, where did you go?" Cindy's mother kept the same phone number for years hoping to get a call from her missing child.

While Cindy's family agonized over her disappearance, Ream was in and out of prison, mainly for sexual assault against girls and young women.

Cindy's file grew cold, but one detective in East Detroit wasn't ready to give up on her case. Detective Danielle Davis pulled Cindy's file and got to work. Davis was convinced this wasn't a missing person's case and that young Cindy met with foul play.

Just as the investigation into Cindy's disappearance was heating up, Detective Davis left the department, and a new detective, Derek McLaughlin, better known as Mac, was assigned the case. When the file landed on his desk, Mac had a thirteen-year-old daughter, and he became fixated on solving Cindy's disappearance.

Mac looked through all the files, and he came to the same conclusion as Davis—it seemed likely that Cindy was murdered. Mac thought for sure Scott Ream's father, Arthur Nelson Ream, was involved. Mac was frustrated that while he had a suspect, he had almost no evidence to connect Ream to Cindy's case.

Then, in 1998, Linda, Ream's first wife and Scott's mother, informed authorities that Ream had recently been convicted of criminal sexual conduct in the third degree. He had sexually assaulted a fifteen-year-old—Ream was this child's legal guardian. He plied the girl with alcohol and then raped her. Ream was sentenced to serve between four and fifteen years behind bars for criminal sexual conduct.

For the next six years, Mac was convinced Ream was involved in Cindy's disappearance, but he still had no evidence to prove it. That's when an investigator at a Chicago-based interrogation company, Jennifer Leibow, became involved.

Leibow read the case files and called Mac, offering to help him out. They started working on Cindy's case.

On January 3, 2008, more than twenty years after Cindy went missing, authorities announced that fifty-eight-year-old Ream (who was set to be paroled in December of that year) was facing first- and second-degree murder charges in Cindy Zarzycki's case. When this news broke in the press, several women came forward to say that Ream had sexually assaulted them, assaults he would never be charged with.

In 2008, after his trial concluded with a guilty verdict, Ream was under relentless pressure from investigators Mac and Leibow to reveal what happened to Cindy Zarzycki. He eventually gave in and agreed to lead them to the spot where he had concealed Cindy's remains decades earlier.

On July 9, 2008, Ream directed them to a twenty-two-acre plot of land near 23 Mile Road and North Avenue in Macomb Township. The group traveled more than half a mile into a wooded area and over a bridge before Ream pointed to a twenty-by-twenty-foot area near a riverbank and said Cindy was buried in a shallow grave there. Authorities dug and found Cindy's body and her denim purse, which still had her beloved mixtapes inside.

Cindy's remains were examined during a thorough autopsy, but a cause of death could not be determined.

On August 7, 2008, Arthur Nelson Ream was sentenced to life without parole for the murder of Cindy Zarzycki. He appealed the conviction. In 2010, the Court of Appeals upheld his conviction.

While Ream never confessed to abducting or murdering anyone else, police suspect he is responsible for additional murders and disappearances. One member of law enforcement said, "He fits the profile of a psychopath."

In the spring of 2018, law enforcement returned to the Macomb Township location, the same place where Cindy's remains were found a decade earlier.

When they performed the dig in 2018, these were some of the missing girls they were reportedly searching for:

- Thirteen-year-old Cynthia Coon, who vanished in 1970 from the Ann Arbor area.
- Sixteen-year-old Nadine O'Dell, who disappeared from the Inkster/Taylor area in 1974.
- Twelve-year-old Kimberly King of Warren, Michigan. It's worth mentioning that Kim King and Cindy Zarzycki were similar in age and appearance.
- Fifteen-year-old Kim Marie Larrow, who went missing from Canton in 1981.
- Seventeen-year-old Kelly Marie Brownlee, who disappeared after visiting 12 Oaks Mall in Novi in the spring of 1982. Ream may have been installing carpeting at a nearby business when she vanished.

Ream's name was also mentioned regarding the 1972 unsolved murder of seventeen-year-old Donna Serra of St Clair Shores, whose body was found by hunters in Ray Township, Macomb County.

The Macomb County Dig site spanned several acres, and with the time and the crew available, only part of the expansive property could be properly searched. Investigators brought in backhoes and heavy equipment to tackle the terrain. While evidence, including women's handbags and accessories, was recovered from the site, no remains were found. As of this writing, no additional searches of this area are planned.

It's long been thought that Ream had other victims. While he resided and had a business in Macomb County, his work as a carpet and flooring installer sent him on jobs all over the Detroit area, including as far west as Ann Arbor.

After living years longer than he deserved, Arthur Nelson Ream died in prison in August 2024. If Ream had information on the disappearances and murders mentioned here, he took that knowledge to the grave.

The property at 23 Mile and North Avenue is still undeveloped. It's possibly the burial place of several young women, but without additional attention or development of the site, we may never know what secrets it holds.

14
KIM KING
1979

In September 1979, twelve-year-old Kim King, the youngest of the three King girls, was a student at Lincoln Middle School in Warren, Michigan.

If you aren't familiar with Warren, you'll find it at the south end of Macomb County, mostly home to auto workers and their families. It's also a vital manufacturing and technological hub. The General Motors Tech Center dominates the heart of the city on Van Dyke near 13 Mile Road right across from city hall and the library. Warren is also home to the U.S. Army Detroit Arsenal, the U.S. Army Tank Command, and the U.S. Army Lifecycle Management Command. The city has a population of about 130,000, making it the third-largest city in Michigan behind Detroit and Grand Rapids.

Warren is known for its many streets with French and German names like Groesbeck, Dequindre, Gratiot, Van Dyke, and Schoenherr. Most of these roads run roughly north and south while mile roads bisect the city from Eight Mile north to the city border at 14 Mile.

Those mile roads run east to west, and Interstate 696 cuts through the center of the city around 11 Mile Road. Geography is important to Kim's case; as we're going to cover where Kim was staying, where she was seen, and where it's thought she disappeared from, it helps to have an idea of the layout.

At the eastern border of north Warren is the city of Roseville. One of Kim's preferred hangout spots was in Roseville.

Kim had two older sisters, Kathie and Konnie, and their parents divorced a couple of years before her disappearance.

Kim's mother was prone to angry outbursts that sometimes became violent. She lost custody of the girls, which put them with their father, Harold King. Harold may have been the more stable and consistent parent, but his challenges included a criminal record.

Harold moved out of Warren to live in Waterford Township in North Oakland County, taking his three daughters with him. Kim didn't enjoy living in Waterford. She missed her friends in Warren and her grandparents. Kim wanted to be with her friends, and her friends were in Warren. Harold's parents, Kim's grandparents, agreed that Kim could live with them in their house on Dodge Avenue, not far from the intersection of Nine Mile and Hoover.

Harold King still worked in Warren, so he was in the area several times a week. The girls' mother had remarried and lived in Sterling Heights, a bedroom community located just north of Warren.

As summer wound down, Kim started preparing for school. She was enrolled at Lincoln Middle School and had many friends in the area, including Annie Godbout, who lived just across the street from the King home. One afternoon, Kim made plans to sleep over at Annie's house.

Unfortunately, Annie's parents said no to this plan, saying that the girls could not have a sleepover. Not to be deterred, Kim came up with a plan of her own.

She told her grandparents that she was staying over at Annie's house and entered Annie's home. Then Kim slipped out of the back of Annie's house, climbed over the rear fence, and was on her way.

Annie knew of Kim's plan to deceive her grandparents and Annie's parents by sneaking back in later. It's thought that when Kim crept away from Annie's house, she was headed east—to Gratiot Avenue.

In the 1970s and 1980s, Gratiot Avenue was a big hangout. People cruised Gratiot, making it a place to see and be seen, get behind the wheel of your fine Detroit steel, and go for a ride. It was a good time. People were out cruising up and down the avenue.

Gratiot Avenue is an eight-lane road with a boulevard in the middle. The road cuts through East Detroit and goes north into Roseville and up to Clinton Township. It may have been six lanes in 1979 with parking along the curb, but either way, it was a nice big road to cruise on.

Kim, despite her tender age, wanted to hang out on Gratiot Avenue. Kim wanted to see and be seen. One of her favorite hangouts was at the White Castle restaurant on Gratiot near 11 Mile Road in Roseville.

Kim's older sisters, who she was close with, were horrified that she was out hitchhiking, cruising, hanging with people she didn't know. They told her this was unsafe. You are putting yourself at risk. Please do not do this. But Kim would not be dissuaded.

Her friends later told the authorities Kim made plans to sleep over and then told the friend in question that she'd see them in a few hours, slipping out of the house to go hang out along Gratiot. Sometimes the friends would sneak out with Kim and they would make the walk east to Gratiot together.

When Kim explained her plan to Annie that night, that she would sneak out and sneak back in later, Kim said she was going to see her sister Kathie.

Kathie planned to drive their dad to his job in Warren and then take his car to pick up Kim and see a movie. Unfortunately, Harold King told Kathie she couldn't take the car that night.

The King home in Waterford did not have a phone. So, Kathie went to a neighbor's house to call her sister Konnie and tell Konnie that if Kim called to tell her sorry, she couldn't pick her up. Eventually, Kim did phone Konnie. Kim was disappointed when she heard that Kathie couldn't pick her up.

Konnie asked Kim where she was calling from, and Kim said she was at a filling station at the corner of Nine Mile Road and Hoover near their grandparents' home.

Konnie told Kim, "Please, go back home." Konnie also asked her what she was doing out at that time of night alone, and Kim told Konnie she was spending the night across the street from their grandmother's home with her friend Annie.

Konnie said, "Please then go back there right now." Kim promised Konnie that she was headed back to Annie's. This was the last time anyone saw or spoke to Kim King.

In retrospect, neither Kathie nor Konnie believed Kim called from the filling station. They later speculated that Kim was likely with someone, perhaps a new "friend," and placed the call from the White Castle restaurant in Roseville.

On Sunday morning, when Kim hadn't returned to Annie's house, the alarm was raised. Annie explained to her parents and later Kim's grandparents what had happened.

Kim's grandparents immediately started making calls trying to locate Kim.

According to a May 2018 story in the *Detroit Free Press*, Kim's sister Kathie and her friend Tina Puckett used markers and photos of Kim to make missing fliers and then spent weeks going up and down Gratiot Avenue posting the fliers and showing Kim's picture to everyone they could in the hopes of finding her.

In the immediate aftermath of her disappearance, Warren police looked at Kim's mother and her husband, suspecting them of involvement in Kim's case.

To be fair, police didn't look too hard for the missing almost thirteen-year-old, if they looked at all. Not in 1979. Kim was written off as a runaway. One of Kim's older sisters had a pattern of running away, so Kim must have done the same.

Kim's sisters pleaded for more attention to her case. Her sister Konnie said, "We tried to express that to the police over and over again. She just would not leave us worrying. I know she would not do that to us." Kim would have contacted Konnie or Kathie; she was close to her sisters.

Police file photos of Kim King. *Author's collection.*

The sisters' concerns were shrugged off. Days passed, and then the runaway aspect didn't look as likely.

Some theorized that since Kim's parents had an ugly divorce and her mom lost custody, maybe it was a power play between the parents, but it wasn't.

Kim was a twelve-year-old girl, a child, and she was missing despite her family's fervent hopes that Kim struck out on her own. Maybe she'd headed to Texas to stay with her cousins or was crashing locally on a friend's sofa.

It wasn't the case. Kim King was gone.

Meanwhile, students at Lincoln Middle School were wondering where Kim went, and rumors were flying that she'd run off to Waterford and was staying with someone there.

If Kim were in Waterford, it would place her not too far from her sisters. Other rumors brought up that Kim liked to run with an older crowd—not just high school boys but high school boys with cars.

Kim's two favorite hangouts were the White Castle restaurant on Gratiot near 11 Mile and an arcade on Eight Mile near Schoenherr. Both locations were checked for Kim on Sunday the sixteenth, but there was no sign of her. The arcade on Eight Mile, Wizzards, was a popular hangout from the late 1970s to the 1990s.

In the days before home gaming systems, teens and young adults hung out at arcades. While teens and young adults today spend time at the local coffeehouse, just like cruising Gratiot, being at the arcade was another way to see and be seen. Kim's sisters didn't think Kim had run off. Not really. While the relationship between the girls and their parents could be challenging, the three sisters stuck together.

Kim would've called. She would've called one of them to say where she was and tell them that she was OK. But Kim never called. In early 1980, months after she vanished, there were reports that Kim had colored her light brown hair to a darker shade and was using the name Tracy. Kim/Tracy was seen up and down Gratiot during the winter and spring of 1980. But when friends, family, or police showed up where she'd been, Kim/Tracy was gone.

In March, investigators finally caught up with Kim/Tracy. It was determined that while Tracy looked a lot like Kim—well, she looked like Kim with dark hair—she was not Kim. The news was heartbreaking to those who held out hope that their girl was still running around and could be found and returned to them safely. When they learned "Tracy" was not Kim, Warren police decided it was time to issue polygraphs.

Back in 1980, polygraphs were viewed in a favorable light. The family was issued polygraphs, but there didn't appear to be any red flags pointing the way to Kim.

Kim's last known location was Annie's house on Dodge Avenue in Warren. Kim told her sister she was calling from a pay phone on Nine Mile Road, a block or two from Annie's house and her grandparents' house.

Police file notes on Kim's case circa 1980. *Author's collection.*

What if Kim lied? What if she wasn't at the pay phone at the corner? What if she'd gone down to Eight Mile Road to Wizzards or up to her favorite fast-food place and made the call from there? Not having this key piece of information, the where to launch a search or a canvass, made Kim's case that much harder to pursue. All investigators had to work with was the ever-changing crowd she ran with on Gratiot Avenue.

Even then, her friends knew only people's first names or had met someone once or twice, but there wasn't a lot of information to start with. Plus, the police weren't talking to Kim's friends. Warren police didn't do a thorough investigation into her case at the time.

To give you an idea of the quality of the initial investigation into Kim's disappearance, Annie, the friend who Kim was supposed to spend the night with, was interviewed by police in 1989, ten years after Kim vanished. Kim's sisters were open about their frustration with the initial response to her case, and they were also open about the help and work done more recently by Warren police, for which they are grateful. As of 2019, familial DNA had been collected along with Kim's dental records.

By 1981, Kim's case was cold, but in March 1983, a journalism student at Columbia University wrote a piece about Kim's disappearance. This brought new attention to her case, nationwide attention, and something shook loose.

In April 1983, a letter arrived at the Roseville Police Department. The handwritten letter contained a confession and a hand-drawn map saying that Kim's remains could be found in a field in northern Macomb County in Shelby Township.

Looking back at this letter through a twenty-first-century lens, it would be nice to know if the flap on the envelope or the stamp was ever swabbed for DNA. Unfortunately, only a photocopy of the letter and envelope exists. The original was misplaced decades ago.

While a search team was assembled and permission sought to access the area, the note was sent to the crime lab for fingerprinting. On April 22, a team descended on the parcel—searchers, cadaver dogs, the works. They were there for three days, but they didn't find anything related to Kim King.

The search of the Shelby Township property in 1983 brought no answers. The land was developed over the last forty years, and no sight or sign of Kim King, or any other missing girl, was discovered there.

In October 1984, Kim's eighteenth birthday came and went. She was now a missing adult.

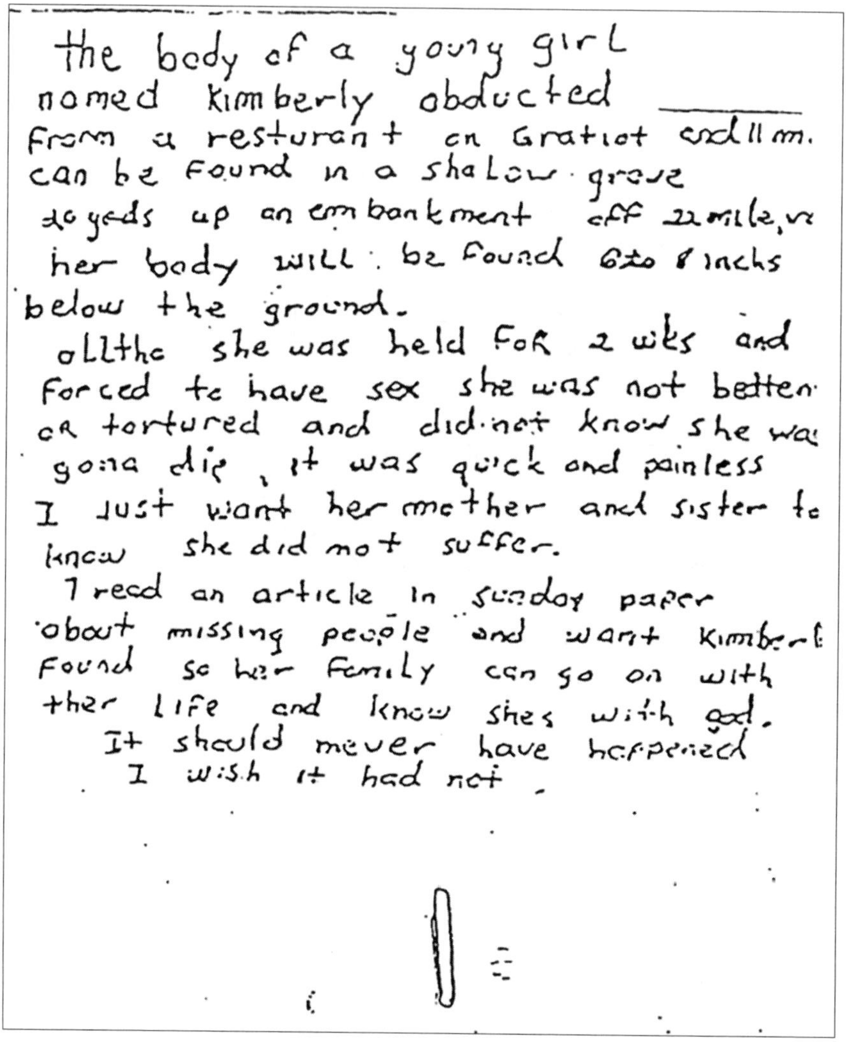

the body of a young girl
named Kimberly abducted ______
from a resturant on Gratiot and 11 m.
can be found in a shalow grave
20 yrds up an embankment off 22 mile, rd
her body will be found 6 to 8 inchs
below the ground.
allthe she was held for 2 wks and
forced to have sex she was not beaten
or tortured and did not know she was
gona die, it was quick and painless
I just want her mother and sister to
know she did not suffer.
I read an article in sunday paper
about missing people and want Kimberly
found so her family can go on with
ther life and know shes with god.
It should never have happened
I wish it had not.

Aside from occasional mentions of Kim's name alongside victims of the Oakland County Child Killer, her case was largely forgotten, until the Macomb County Dig in 2018.

Kim's sister Konnie Beyma commented in 2018 that "it would mean a great deal to bring her remains home."

There has been little movement in Kim's case since the Macomb Township Dig. Warren police seem convinced that Arthur Nelson Ream, who died in prison in 2024 and is discussed in the Macomb County Dig chapter, was responsible for Kim's disappearance. Kim's sisters aren't

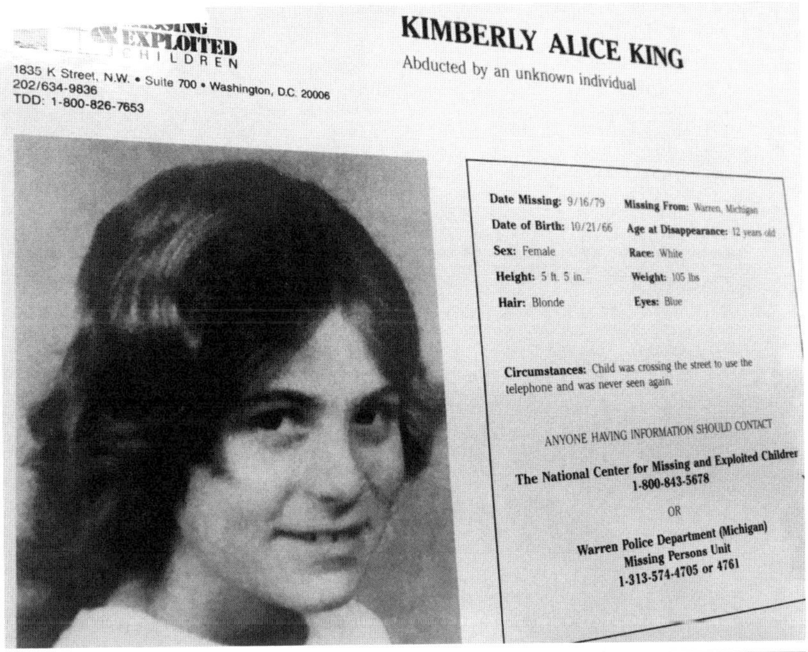

EXPLOITED CHILDREN
1835 K Street, N.W. • Suite 700 • Washington, D.C. 20006
202/634-9836
TDD: 1-800-826-7653

KIMBERLY ALICE KING
Abducted by an unknown individual

Date Missing: 9/16/79 **Missing From:** Warren, Michigan
Date of Birth: 10/21/66 **Age at Disappearance:** 12 years old
Sex: Female **Race:** White
Height: 5 ft. 5 in. **Weight:** 105 lbs
Hair: Blonde **Eyes:** Blue

Circumstances: Child was crossing the street to use the telephone and was never seen again.

ANYONE HAVING INFORMATION SHOULD CONTACT

The National Center for Missing and Exploited Children
1-800-843-5678

OR

Warren Police Department (Michigan)
Missing Persons Unit
1-313-574-4705 or 4761

Opposite: A copy of the letter sent to law enforcement claiming knowledge of Kim King's kidnapping and murder. *Author's collection.*

Above: Flyer for Kim King. *Created by the National Center for Missing and Exploited Children.*

Right: Age progression photo of Kim King. *National Center for Missing and Exploited Children.*

as certain. They're hopeful that as more people learn about Kim's case someone will come forward with information that leads to her remains.

In the years after Kim disappeared, her grandmother purchased two burial plots: one for her and one for Kim. It sits empty, waiting for Kim to finally return to her grandmother, where she can be safe.

If you have information on the disappearance of Kim King, contact Warren Police Detective Bureau at 586-574-4700.

15

KIM LARROW

1981

June 8, 1981, was a warm sunny day with temperatures headed for eighty-two degrees when fifteen-year-old Kim Marie Larrow left her mother's home on Beaufort Street in Canton, Michigan, hoping to meet up with friends at the local ice cream parlor.

Kim didn't live in Canton; she was just there for a couple of weeks to see her mom. She'd only been in town for a few days and didn't have a social circle in Canton to hang out with. Kim was hoping to meet people and make some friends in the area.

After her parents' divorce, she stayed with her father in the little town of Dundee, Michigan, so she could remain in school and with her friends. Her father, Arnold Larrow, owned a bar, Arnie's Party Pack,[36] where Kim sometimes worked or helped out.

Kim's parents had divorced a year or two earlier, and Kim was struggling with the changes. In one notable incident, she took off with a friend and headed for Florida. It wasn't long before she returned home. Kim was a sweet kid and a lot like other kids her age. She drank sometimes, was curious about marijuana, and was interested in boys.

Canton, a sprawling suburban development west of Detroit, was semirural in the early 1980s. While there were neighborhoods and strip malls, there were also working farms and a small airport; it was not the bustling suburb you see today.

On the day she vanished, Kim told her mother she was going to Stroh's ice cream parlor and told a friend she was heading to Haggerty Field near Hines Park to hang out.

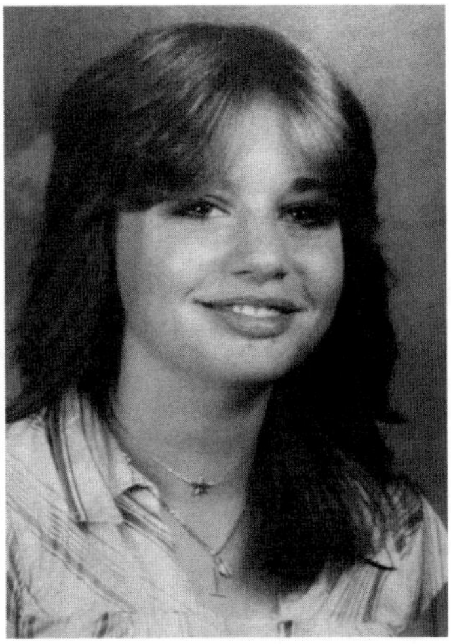

Kim Marie Larrow. Missing since 1981. *Author's collection.*

Like many other landmarks in and around Detroit, Hines Park is named for an automotive innovator. Edward Hines was the first road commissioner of Wayne County. Hines was responsible for creating the "center line" on the road. He got the idea after seeing a leaking milk truck head down a busy street, neatly carving it in half with a trail of spilled product. This breakthrough created different paths for traffic traveling in opposing directions.

Hines also believed in beautifying roads, eliminating billboards, and creating parks. Hines Park was named in his honor. Hines Park probably isn't what you're thinking of when you picture a park. Hines Park straddles a winding road, almost twenty miles long, which runs a leisurely northwest course from Dearborn to Northville. It doesn't touch Canton, and Haggerty Field, rumored to be her destination, was five miles from Kim's home with her mother that summer.

Frustratingly there isn't much information about Kim's story. Her mother didn't report Kim missing until three days after she disappeared. At that point, because Kim had a history of running away, Canton police treated her case like that of a runaway. Investigators had no way of knowing that nearly forty-odd years later her disappearance would be Canton's oldest unsolved case.

Kim's mother, Lucy Larrow, was at work the day Kim vanished. At the time, Larrow was employed by Ford Motor Company at the Rawsonville Ford Plant in Ypsilanti.

While a search was conducted of Kim's room at her mother's house, DNA evidence wasn't collected. Kim vanished in the days before DNA was commonly known.

Kim was new to Canton; there were no school friends to check with as to her whereabouts. It cannot be confirmed that Kim made it to the ice cream parlor that day. Nor can we confirm that she arrived at Haggerty Field. Long after she went missing, police realized that the teen was more than just a runaway, and they brought in cadaver dogs to search through Hines Park.

Kim's cousin Robert Cooper, a retired police officer, and her older half siblings, Brandon and Andrea, advocated for Kim and did what they could to keep her disappearance in the public eye.

At one point, the FBI was brought in to consult with Canton police. Unfortunately, their support of the investigation did not lead to a resolution.

One of the hurdles in Kim's case, aside from her being treated like a runaway instead of the victim of a crime, is an issue with her photos. The picture most shared is of Kim with reddish-blond hair wearing a white top with pastel flowers. This photo was on the cover of the *Canton Observer* in 2008. Unfortunately, that wasn't the most recent picture of her.

A more recent photo shows a pretty young woman with sandy-blond hair, wearing a bit of makeup and jewelry. Kim looks like a young adult, whereas the photo most often circulated concerning her disappearance shows a much younger Kim Larrow.

As the 1980s progressed, the city of Canton grew, and Kim's file, while not forgotten, became dusty. Arnold Larrow hired a private investigator to look for his missing daughter, but the PI came up empty. Arnie Larrow died in 2005, never knowing what happened to Kim.

According to Canton police, Kim had no social security number and was too young for a driver's license. This meant they couldn't track her via work history.

As reported in the *Canton Observer*, Kim's mother, Lucy, retired to Arizona. When Canton police took another look at Kim's case in the late 2010s, they struggled to connect with Lucy Larrow, although they attempted to reach her multiple times.

Kim's cousin Robert Cooper told the *Canton Observer* in 2008 that Lucy Larrow told him to "drop it" when he asked her about Kim's disappearance.

Aside from infrequent mentions of Kim's name in press stories about cold cases or mentions on missing persons websites, her case was largely forgotten, until the Macomb County Dig.

Investigators considered whether Kim Larrow could be a victim of suspected serial killer Arthur Nelson Ream. Ream, who died in prison in the fall of 2024, was serving a life sentence for the 1986 murder of thirteen-year-old Cindy Zarzycki. Arthur Ream has been looked at in Kim's case, but until Kim is recovered, it's hard to know which direction investigators should pursue.

As of 2024, Kim's family, especially her older brother, Brandon Headley, have not given up hope that Kim can be found. Headley remains in close contact with investigators in Canton. If you have information on the disappearance of Kim Larrow, contact Canton police at 734-374-5400.

16

KELLIE MARIE BROWNLEE

1982

On May 20, 1982, Kellie Marie Brownlee was a girl on a mission. She was seventeen years old, pretty, and dark-haired. Since things at home could best be described as difficult, she was staying with her boyfriend, Mark Graves.

That morning, Kellie traded in her jeans and khaki jacket for white pants and a peach top; she was going to spend the day at 12 Oaks Mall in Novi searching for a summer job. Kellie wanted to get her applications in before the other kids, maybe even snag a job that day, so she could work and save her money all summer.

Mark was worried when Kellie didn't return to the Graves home that night. He picked up the phone and started calling around. No one had seen or heard from Kellie.

To get to the mall on her own without a car, it was likely that Kellie hitched a ride. With Kellie not returning to his home that night, Mark asked Kellie's friend Carrie to call Kellie's mom and see if she was there. Despite the tension at home, Kellie loved her mom, Loretta, and stayed in close contact with her.

Loretta said that she hadn't heard from Kellie, and when Carrie told her that Kellie was missing, Loretta's heart sank.

More phone calls to friends and neighbors revealed that the mother of one of Kellie's friends saw Kellie at the mall that morning. Kellie happily told the mom that she'd applied at Winkelman's, Brooks, and Alberts. The mom offered Kellie a lift home, but Kellie declined, saying that she wanted to apply at more stores. The two parted ways. This was the last confirmed sighting of Kellie, a brunette with the Farrah Fawcett hair.

When police interviewed people she'd interacted with at 12 Oaks Mall, they reported that Kellie seemed to be in good spirits and she was alone. Kellie listed her mother's address in West Bloomfield as her home address on job applications, even though she was staying with her boyfriend.

Let's pause here a minute: Why was Kellie staying with her boyfriend? Who thought this was a good idea, a seventeen-year-old girl staying with her eighteen-year-old boyfriend? Her mother was OK with the situation because Kellie's home life wasn't ideal. The Graves family gave her a safe place to stay.

Kellie's mother, Loretta, married Paul Brownlee in 1970, when Kellie was six years old. Paul helped raise Kellie and her older sister, Kim.

When Kim became a teenager, there were problems. Kellie accused Paul of inappropriate behavior, touching and possibly worse. Friends reported seeing Kellie with bruises.

In 1977, Kellie's older sister, Kim, moved to California to live with their biological father. Kellie stayed in Michigan with her mother and stepfather.

Kellie loved her mother and wanted to be with her, but Paul's presence made things difficult.

Loretta was in nursing school, and once she finished, hopefully by the end of 1982, word was that she planned to leave Paul and take Kellie with her. Loretta asked Kellie to hold on just a little longer.

Kellie tried to hold on as her mother asked. She retreated to a friend's house or Mark's house when things at home were tense. Loretta didn't work outside the home, leaving her with no way to support herself and her daughter. Some people think Kellie's plan to find work at the mall was to hasten her departure from the Brownlee home.

Police investigated the whereabouts of Paul Brownlee on the day Kellie disappeared. Paul said he'd gone to the gym to work out and then visited the cemetery, located directly across the street from 12 Oaks Mall, to pay his respects to Loretta's father, his father-in-law. According to a May 2000 story in the *Detroit Free Press*, Paul said that he didn't see Kellie that day. Loretta was interviewed by the police, and she was cleared. Police also spoke with and ruled out Kellie's boyfriend, Mark Graves.

Kellie wasn't perfect; rumor has it that she'd been expelled from an all-girls Catholic high school for a prank involving graffiti. Kelle smoked cigarettes, and she liked to party, listen to Ozzy Osbourne, and hang with her friends. In all honesty, this sounds like typical teen behavior for the time.

Kellie didn't appear to have been in trouble with the law or a problem student at her new school in Walled Lake.

In June 1982, Paul Brownlee offered a $1,000 reward for information leading to the safe return of Kellie.

Paul Brownlee may not have been involved in Kellie's disappearance, but he was a person of interest in her case. Paul called police to report that he'd received a tip—Kellie had been seen at a local ice cream parlor in the company of two men. The tip from Paul led nowhere.

What appeared to be a simple missing person's case took a strange turn. We have proof that a violent sexual sadist was in the Novi area around the time Kellie vanished. His name? James Mitchell Debardeleben.

Debardeleben, who went by Mike, was a counterfeiter with a long criminal history. One of his favorite tricks was stopping at malls located near freeways and passing counterfeit bills there.

Twelve Oaks Mall is located just off Interstate 96, which cuts a westerly path across Michigan.

Debardeleben had a long and disturbing history. He was sixteen when he violently assaulted his mother in 1956. Later that year, he was charged with possession of a firearm. He dropped out of school and enlisted in the Air Force. It didn't take long for Debardeleben to get in trouble, and he was court-martialed for disorderly behavior. The Air Force sentenced him to eight weeks in the stockade. He was dishonorably discharged at age eighteen and went to live with relatives in Texas. He re-enrolled in high school but was expelled within months.

Debardeleben married and divorced before he was twenty. He fathered at least three children: one was stillborn, and one, a daughter, Beth. A third child was given up for adoption at his insistence.

By 1980, the Secret Service was looking at him for his mall pass scheme. He would visit a shopping mall with a wad of counterfeit twenty-dollar bills. He would visit several stores and buy one small item at each; he would pay for the item with a fake bill and receive good cash in return.

In 1982, law enforcement traced some of his money to stores at 12 Oaks Mall. Is it possible that Kellie, the pretty dark-haired high school student, crossed his path?

While Debardeleben was never charged with murder, he was a known sexual sadist with a reputation for picking up hitchhikers and is suspected in but was never charged for at least two murders. When the law finally caught up with him, he received a sentence of 375 years to be served at a federal prison in North Carolina.

While in prison, Debardeleben befriended several serial murderers and rapists and shared detailed stories about his crimes. He died of pneumonia while incarcerated at a federal prison back in 2011.

During their investigation of Debardeleben, authorities uncovered dozens of photographs of women who were victims of his sexual assaults. Those photographs were shared with West Bloomfield police, who in turn showed the photos to Kellie's mother to see if she recognized her daughter. Eventually, Debardeleben was ruled out in Kellie's case, but his name still comes up from time to time.

In August 1982, West Bloomfield police asked Paul Brownlee to take a polygraph, but he refused. Brownlee hired an attorney to handle further contact between himself and law enforcement.

In 1991, almost a decade after Kellie vanished, Paul Brownlee paid a visit to the West Bloomfield police. He had avoided talking with them for years, but here he was, saying that he had a lead for investigators. He showed police a catalogue from a Michigan-based retail chain, and in the catalogue was a dark-haired girl in a swimsuit.

Paul Brownlee was convinced that the girl in the catalogue was Kellie. He asked the police to investigate the lead. The girl Brownlee was sure was Kellie was twelve years old. In 1991, Kellie would have been twenty-six. Police asked him again where he was the day Kellie vanished. Paul walked out of the station without answering additional questions.

Brownlee has never been charged in her case, nor has he been cleared. While there are multiple theories in Kellie's case, we can't say if she was picked up by the wrong guy, attacked by her stepfather, or left the area on her own.

Age progression photo of Kellie Brownlee. *National Center for Missing and Exploited Children.*

Kellie's mother finished nursing school and left Paul Brownlee in 1985, getting the divorce Kellie had waited for. Both Kellie's mother and Paul Brownlee have passed away.

Aside from infrequent mentions of Kellie's name in press stories about cold cases or mentions on missing persons websites, her case was mostly forgotten, until the Macomb County Dig.

Investigators considered whether Kellie Brownlee could be a victim of suspected serial killer Arthur Nelson Ream. Ream, who died in prison in the fall of 2024, was serving a life sentence for the 1986 murder of thirteen-year-old Cindy Zarzycki. Arthur Ream has been looked at in Kellie's case, but until she is recovered, it's hard to know which direction investigators should pursue.

West Bloomfield Police are still working on Kellie's case.

NOTES

1. Here and throughout, an asterisk indicates the use of pseudonyms.
2. Kayla Clarke, "Who Killed Debra Rentschler? Eighteen-Year-Old Found Dead in Farmington Snowbank on Christmas 42 Years Ago," ClickOnDetroit, January 4, 2023, https://www.clickondetroit.com/news/local/2023/01/04/who-killed-debra-rentschler-18-year-old-found-dead-in-farmington-snowbank-on-christmas-42-years-ago/.
3. *Detroit Free Press*, April 24, 1981, https://www.newspapers.com/image/98697741/.
4. "Woman's Body Found in Area Parking Lot," *Farmington Observer*, January 1, 1981, https://history.farmlib.org/localhist/npageturn.cgi?id=1762&sequence=4.
5. *Detroit Free Press*, December 31, 1991, https://www.newspapers.com/image/100382097/.
6. *Detroit Free Press*, December 25, 1991, https://www.newspapers.com/image/100380097.
7. Pann v. Warren, Justia U.S. Law, https://law.justia.com/cases/federal/district-courts/michigan/miedce/5:2008cv13806/233171/22/.
8. *Pann v. Warren.*
9. *Detroit Free Press*, January 31, 1992, https://www.newspapers.com/image/99605805/.
10. *Detroit Free Press*, July 12, 1992, https://www.newspapers.com/image/99994782/.
11. *Detroit Free Press*, December 15, 1992, https://www.newspapers.com/image/99221755/.

12. *Times Herald*, December 15, 1992, https://www.newspapers.com/image/211237675/.
13. *Detroit Free Press*, December 18, 1992, https://www.newspapers.com/image/99222297/.
14. *Detroit Free Press*, January 26, 1995, https://www.newspapers.com/image/99217445/.
15. *Detroit Free Press*, March 16, 1993, https://www.newspapers.com/image/97997713/.
16. *Detroit Free Press*, October 23, 1994, https://www.newspapers.com/image/98935930/.
17. *Detroit Free Press*, January 26, 1995, https://www.newspapers.com/image/99217439/.
18. *Detroit Free Press*, September 15, 1995, https://www.newspapers.com/image/99255597/.
19. *Detroit Free Press*, April 23, 1996, https://www.newspapers.com/image/99372218/.
20. *Detroit Free Press*, January 15, 1997, https://www.newspapers.com/image/99365753/.
21. *Detroit Free Press*, April 23, 1996, https://www.newspapers.com/image/99372218/.
22. *Detroit Free Press*, January 30, 2001, https://www.newspapers.com/image/361646217/.
23. *Detroit Free Press*, January 25, 2001, https://www.newspapers.com/image/361627806/.
24. "The Murder of Garnet Lennox: A Car in East Detroit," *The Fall Line*, December 7, 2022, https://www.thefalllinepodcast.com/episodes/2022/12/7/the-murder-of-garnet-lennox-a-car-in-east-detroit.
25. *Atlanta Constitution*, June 4, 1994, https://www.newspapers.com/image/403059705/.
26. "Pontiac Police Department Closes: Oakland County Sheriff's Department to Take Over," ClickOnDetroit, August 1, 2011, https://www.clickondetroit.com/news/2011/08/01/pontiac-police-department-closes/.
27. *Detroit Free Press*, July 13, 1990, https://www.newspapers.com/image/100005777/.
28. *Detroit Free Press*, July 13, 1990, https://www.newspapers.com/image/100005777/.
29. *Detroit Free Press*, July 13, 1990, https://www.newspapers.com/image/100005777/.

30. *Macomb Daily*, July 1, 2006, https://www.macombdaily.com/2006/07/01/court-wont-restore-mount-clemens-police/.
31. "Nicholas Cottrell Gets Up to Fifty Years in Prison in Death of Westland Teen Carlee Morse," MLive, February 4, 2011, https://www.mlive.com/news/detroit/2011/02/nicholas_cottrell_gets_up_to_5.html.
32. *Detroit Free Press*, February 4, 2011, https://www.newspapers.com/image/364066920/.
33. *Detroit Free Press*, February 4, 2011, https://www.newspapers.com/image/364066920/?clipping_id=19555590.
34. "Man Arraigned After Oakland County Sheriff Mike Bouchard Caught Him Impersonating a Cop," WXYZ Detroit, February 8, 2020, https://www.wxyz.com/news/man-arraigned-after-caught-by-oakland-county-sheriff-mike-bouchard-impersonating-a-police-officer.
35. "Scott Christopher 'Shark' Ream," Find a Grave, https://www.findagrave.com/memorial/108101552/scott-christopher-ream.
36. "Arnold Arthur 'Arnie' Larrow Jr.," Find a Grave, https://www.findagrave.com/memorial/50203573/arnold-arthur-larrow.

ABOUT THE AUTHOR

Nina Innsted is the creator, writer, and voice behind *Already Gone*, a gripping true crime podcast launched in 2016, dedicated to uncovering compelling stories from Michigan and the Great Lakes region. A multitalented force in the industry, she has worked as a producer, researcher, writer, and voice talent on major projects, including *Up and Vanished* "The Trial of Ryan Duke." Her collaboration with Tenderfoot TV on *Up and Vanished* earned an Ambie Award in 2023.

Beyond podcasting, Nina is a sought-after public speaker, regularly presenting at industry events and fundraisers such as AdvocacyCon and CrimeStoppers.

She is also a credentialed victim's advocate and the media coordinator for Missing in Michigan, a nonprofit that supports families of missing persons.

A proud Metro Detroit native, Nina lives with her husband and two children. Follow her on Instagram and Threads: @NinaInnsted.